# THE SIGN OF JONAH IN THE THEOLOGY

# OF THE EVANGELISTS AND Q

# STUDIES IN BIBLICAL THEOLOGY

A series of monographs designed to provide clergy and laymen with the best work in biblical scholarship both in this country and abroad

*Advisory Editors:*

STUDIES IN BIBLICAL THEOLOGY

Second Series · 18

# THE SIGN OF JONAH
## In the Theology of the Evangelists and Q

RICHARD ALAN EDWARDS

ALEC R. ALLENSON INC.
635 EAST OGDEN AVENUE
NAPERVILLE, ILL.

BS
600.2
.S824

ISBN 0-8401-3068-6

Published by Alec R. Allenson Inc.
Naperville, Ill.
Printed in Great Britain

TO JUNE

# CONTENTS

# PREFACE

AS THE TITLE indicates, this study is an example of redaction criticism at work on one small portion of the synoptic tradition. It is my hope that it will be useful not only as an attempt to solve the problem of the Sign of Jonah but also as an introduction to various styles of biblical analysis.

Most of the material presented here was written during the academic year 1967–8 at the Divinity School of the University of Chicago. Part of chapter II has appeared as an article, 'The Eschatological Correlative as a *Gattung* in the New Testament', in *Zeitschrift für die neutestamentliche Wissenschaft* 60 (1969), pp. 9–20.

I would like to express my deep appreciation to Dr Norman Perrin for his sage guidance and careful criticism as the work proceeded. His assistance and encouragement were invaluable. A special note of thanks also to my fellow students, Vernon Robbins and Dennis Duling, for their help at many points along the way, and also to Karen Carlson for her help in preparing the indexes.

R. A. EDWARDS

# PREFACE

# ABBREVIATIONS

| | |
|---|---|
| ASNU | Acta Seminarii Neotestamentici Upsaliensis, Uppsala: C. W. K. Gleerup |
| *ExpT* | *Expository Times,* Edinburgh |
| FRLANT | Forschungen zur Religion und Literatur des Alten und Neuen Testaments, Göttingen: Vandenhoeck und Ruprecht |
| *HTR* | *Harvard Theological Review,* Cambridge, Mass. |
| *JAAR* | *Journal of the American Academy of Religion,* Chambersburg, Pa. |
| *JBL* | *Journal of Biblical Literature,* Philadelphia |
| *JTS* | *Journal of Theological Studies,* Oxford |
| NTL | New Testament Library, London: SCM Press, and Philadelphia: Westminster Press |
| *NTS* | *New Testament Studies,* Cambridge |
| SBT | Studies in Biblical Theology, London: SCM Press, and Naperville, Ill.: Allenson |
| *SJT* | *Scottish Journal of Theology,* Edinburgh |
| *TDNT* | *Theological Dictionary of the New Testament,* trans. G. W. Bromiley from *TWNT*, Grand Rapids, Michigan: Eerdmans, 1964ff. |
| *TWNT* | *Theologisches Wörterbuch zum Neuen Testament,* ed. G. Kittel, Stuttgart: W. Kohlhammer, 1933ff. |
| *ZThK* | *Zeitschrift für Theologie und Kirche,* Tübingen |

# I

## A HISTORY OF CRITICISM AND A
## STATEMENT OF METHOD

### THE PROBLEM

*A Description of the Sign of Jonah Pericopes and Related Problems*

THERE ARE few synoptic pericopes which have caused more difficulties than the Sign of Jonah. The phrase 'sign of Jonah' appears three times in the New Testament: twice in Matthew, at 12.39 and 16.4, and once in Luke at 11.29. Although Mark does not record this phrase, he does have a report of the refusal of a sign (Mark 8.11–13) which is, in part, closely related to the Sign of Jonah reports in Matthew and Luke. Thus, there are four synoptic passages which will demand our consideration in the following study.

The central problem is raised by the lack of agreement between Matthew and Luke in their respective explanations of the meaning of the Sign of Jonah. Luke 11.30 reads: 'For just as Jonah was a sign to the Ninevites, so the Son of Man will be to this generation.' In his parallel passage (12.40) Matthew records: 'For just as Jonah was in the belly of the fish three days and three nights, so the Son of Man will be in the heart of the earth three days and three nights.' Even though Matthew and Luke share certain features, the obvious differences between Matthew and Luke raise a question about the correct, and perhaps original, meaning of the Sign of Jonah.

In the verses which follow the explanations, Matthew and Luke record a similar pair of sayings (Matt. 12.41f; Luke 11.31f.), but the *order* of the saying differs.

Finally, Matt. 16.1–4, which also refers to the sign of Jonah, does not contain an explanation, as does Matthew 12.40, but reports a saying about 'signs of the times' (16.2b–3) before the

Sign of Jonah saying in 16.4. This limited doublet in Matthew must therefore also be considered.

As an example of the wide variety of questions which have been raised about the Sign of Jonah, the following report of an article by Anton Vögtle[1] is presented. Vögtle's article is a very complete and comprehensive survey of previous research on this problem and affords an excellent insight to the multitudinous questions raised by synoptic scholars in the past hundred years. Vögtle has arranged the many suggestions and questions by subject matter in order to concentrate attention upon related solutions and not upon the men who have proposed them. Thus his work serves as an introduction to the scope and complexity of the problem. His own solution to the problem will be presented later in this chapter.

Vögtle's article is divided into six sections: Parts One, Two and Three discuss specific issues which these three synoptic passages have raised about the Sign of Jonah. In Part Four the literary-critical solution is outlined and in Part Five the tradition-history contribution is stated. Vögtle's contribution is at the end of Part Five, where he makes use of the insights of the tradition-history approach and reaches a practical solution based on the principles of form criticism. Part Six is a summary.

Part One is divided into the four issues which scholars have isolated as the central ones. First is the basic problem of the divergence of the tradition. If there are not two separate events being reported, what is the reason for the divergence which exists between Mark and Matthew-Luke? Does Mark want to express the enigmatic character of the response, assuming that Jesus' reply about the Sign of Jonah is an alternative to simply saying 'No'? Why then do Matthew and Luke differ? Is it a question of one representing Q and the other an earlier source? Is it that there really is no difference, that both Matthew and Luke intend to say the same thing? Secondly, can we find a more positive solution by an analysis of the context? The comparison sayings which follow the Sign of Jonah are often used by exegetes to supply an answer to the question of the meaning of the sign. But this 'double saying' presents problems of its own: is the centre of concern Jesus' appearance or his preaching? If preaching, why the refer-

---

[1] Anton Vögtle, 'Der Spruch vom Jonaszeichen', in *Synoptische Studien*: *Alfred Wikenhauser zum siebzigsten Geburtstag am 22. Februar 1953 dargebracht vom Freunden, Kollegen und Schülern* (1953), pp. 230–77.

ence to Solomon? Was the 'double saying' a later addition because of the catchword Jonah? Thirdly, what is the function of the Son of Man in this saying? Opinions diverge widely here, some preferring to assert the authenticity of Luke 11.30 because it is a future Son of Man saying, others asserting that the Son of Man portion of the saying illustrates its lateness. The easiest solution is to claim that Jesus was speaking in riddles and that both Matthew and Luke are making the best of an inherently difficult problem. Fourthly, the eschatological issue is merely mentioned by Vögtle as a source of speaking about the prophetic character of Jesus' reference to the future.

Part Two is a detailed statement of the relation between Mark and Matthew-Luke. The Semitic character of Mark's report has often been used to support an argument for Markan priority. Matthew and Luke both show signs of moving away from the Semitic character of the Markan Greek – as well as having the added 'exceptions' and the explanation. Some have suggested that Mark probably knew the phrase εἰ μὴ τὸ σημεῖον 'Ιωνᾶ but dropped it because of its enigmatic quality.

Part Three approaches the problem from the analysis of the word 'sign' and its historical background. What do the Pharisees mean when they ask about a sign? Is it a response to the message about the kingdom of God or a response to the claim of Messiah? Why is it a 'sign from heaven' in some reports? Is the phrase apocalyptic, eschatological or a synonym for God? Most exegetes assume that Jesus is redefining the word sign by giving the answer that he does – his mission does not allow this sort of demand. What is it that makes the Pharisee part of this evil generation? Are signs only to be defined within the context of faith? Does this mean that the answer 'except the sign of Jonah' is really an elaborate 'No' to the Pharisee's demand? Vögtle points out that a solution of this kind is not justified exegetically; there is no indication that 'sign' now has a new meaning. Since sign seems to be some sort of 'wonder', it must be a reference to a 'wonder' in the book of Jonah, viz. the miraculous deliverance from the fish. Vögtle's summary in Part Three asserts that Jesus would not have offered a riddle as a sign. A wonder is demanded and Jesus there-fore refers them to a wonder – a wonder for this immediate genera-tion. Yet, Jesus does not usually make faith dependent on a sign. The suggestion that Jonah is a mistranslation of John has no textual basis and relies exclusively on Luke 11.30, with John as the preacher of repentance. But, Vögtle comments, Jesus' *preaching* could not be construed as a belief-wonder.[2]

Part Four is a more systematic attempt to show how literary criticism has approached the problem and was eventually unable to offer an acceptable solution. First of all, Matthew and Luke are so close that there can be little doubt that they are relying on Q; the similarity runs from specific whole sentences and words to the structure of the complete incident. Luke must be closer to Q, because he connects the refusal to the explanation in a purer catch-word way: σημεῖον in 11.29 and 11.30 and ἡ γενεὰ αὕτη in 11.29 and 11.30. Because Luke has made this connection already, he maintains the double saying in its original order while Matthew must reverse it to keep the continuity. As a result of the emphasis on Luke, source criticism tended to interpret the sign as the repentance-preaching of Jesus or as the mere appearance of Jesus. Luke took over Q because he agreed with Q.[3]

The last major section, Part Five, turns to the tradition-history analysis. Matthew 12.40 must be a reference to the resurrection because death implies a return to life; Jonah is spewed out and Jesus is raised. Since the death is not a 'wonder', the resurrection is the sign. However, others find it a reference to the parousia; Jesus is the world judge who dies and rises. Vögtle is critical of this position because it ignores the specific reference to the death that appears in the quotation from Jonah 2.1. He claims that Matthew has used the quotation as a proof,[4] even though the three days and three nights parallel is inaccurate. Matthew has apparently changed the Q saying. He is more precise about the analogy and removes any doubt about the meaning of the saying. It is possible that 'three days' is simply a way of saying 'a short time'. Matthew has created another messianic scripture proof. It is more likely that Matthew is secondary to Luke.[5]

Vögtle's catalogue of tradition-history interpretations of Luke 11.30 follows.[6] The sign can be the message *and* the action of Jesus, i.e. he is self-authenticating. But now we are back to Mark.

---

[2] *Op. cit.,* pp. 244–7.

[3] *Ibid.,* pp. 248–53.

[4] Cf. Matthew's use (Matt. 21.4–7) of the quotation from Zech. 9.9, in which the details are taken literally, or at least not modified.

[5] Vögtle, 'Jonaszeichen', pp. 253–63.

[6] *Ibid.,* pp. 263–73.

Jesus will rise and appear to this generation as Jonah 'rose' and appeared to the Ninevites. Or, Jesus is the sign when he appears as the judge at the *eschaton*; but then the sign is too late.

It is at this point that Vögtle presents his own suggestion which will be detailed later in this chapter.

Perhaps the simplest solution to this confusion is to assert that the problem lies in our attempting to correlate these passages when they probably represent reports of similar but different events in the life of Jesus. Jesus may have responded in a variety of ways at different times and we are at fault in trying to explain the variety on the basis of an unfounded assumption about their common origin.[7]

Simple though this answer may be, it does violence to the widely accepted recognition of the nature of the synoptic gospels.[8] If we were dealing with a set of chronicles, this solution would indeed be possible. But the gospels stand as the end result of a long period of oral transmission. And, even more crucial, they are not literal or scientific reports, but statements of faith expressed in narrative form. Narrative is not necessarily history. Rather, we must use these documents as sources for the faith of those who transmitted them. They are post-Easter creations and we must approach them as witnesses to the faith of the church, not as accurate descriptions of the life of Jesus.[9]

*Outline of the Thesis*

It is the purpose of this thesis to suggest that there can be a unified though not simple solution to this complex problem. Previously, a method did not exist which could unravel these interwoven strands of material found in this collection of pericopes. The following survey of the research on the Sign of Jonah is basically a report of limited success in certain areas, and a total lack of success in offering a complete answer to the question: What was the Sign of Jonah? It is only now, with the combined efforts of form and redaction criticism, that a comprehensive

---

[7] This solution is suggested by B. Gerhardsson, *Memory and Manuscript: Oral Tradition and Written Transmission in Rabbinic Judaism and Early Christianity* (1961), p. 335.

[8] For a summary statement of the form-critical understanding of the gospels see: Norman Perrin, *Rediscovering the Teaching of Jesus* (1967), pp. 15–53.

[9] *Ibid.*

solution can even be offered. Whether this particular solution will stand the test of time, or not, does not detract from the fact that it is a *comprehensive* answer, something which has not been achieved before.

Chapter I presents a selected history of the interpretation of the Sign of Jonah, emphasizing the methods involved at each stage of the history. The most recent work is outlined and criticized in order to clarify the method which will be used in this thesis, i.e. redaction criticism.

Chapter II is a statement of the theology of the evangelists and Q. If we are to stress the internal consistency of each level of tradition, it is necessary to grasp the overall structure of each. From this basis, the Sign of Jonah can be seen in its proper context.

Chapter III is a proposed history of the tradition of the Sign of Jonah which argues that significant development has taken place, particularly in Q, and that each redactor has indicated his theological *Sitz im Leben* by the way in which he has made use of the tradition which he received.

## A SURVEY OF THE CRITICISM OF THE SIGN OF JONAH AND A STATEMENT OF THE METHOD

### Source Criticism

Source or literary criticism of the synoptic gospels operates upon the assumption that the present form of the first three gospels is the result of the collation of earlier written documents. This conclusion is based upon years of comparative studies of the gospels which sought to explain the variations, as well as the agreements, by seeking the written sources used by each evangelist. The result of this work is the two-document hypothesis: Mark is the basic source for both Matthew and Luke; Matthew and Luke each also used another common source, called Q, which was not known to Mark. The evidence for this conclusion is impressive.[10] Not only does a large part of Mark's gospel appear in Matthew and Luke, the *order* in which Mark is used by Matthew and Luke is strikingly similar.

---

[10] See especially the text and bibliography in Paul Feine, Johannes Behm, and Werner Kümmel, *Introduction to the New Testament*, trans. from the 14th rev. ed. (1966), pp. 50–8, (hereafter cited as Kümmel, *Introduction*).

The evidence for the existence of the second source, Q, consists of the large amount of similar material in Matthew and Luke which has no parallel in Mark. The two-source hypothesis explains this by arguing that Matthew and Luke worked independently and have relied on a common source (*Quelle*) rather than copying from each other. There have been some recent attempts to reject the possibility of a Q source by showing that Luke had access to a copy of Matthew – thus explaining the material common to both. The problems posed by this alternative, however, are even greater than those of the two-source theory, the most obvious difficulty being the question: If Luke did use Matthew as a source, is it conceivable that he would alter in every case (except for the baptism and temptation) each pericope's position in the Markan outline as Matthew arranged it? The two-source theory offers a simpler solution: Matthew and Luke independently use a common sayings-source each in his own unique way. The source critic, in his day, was convinced that a Q *document* must have existed on the basis of the many word-for-word parallels between Matthew and Luke.[11]

Upon this literary evidence was erected the Markan hypothesis which states that Mark, as the source of Matthew and Luke, must be recognized as temporally prior to Matthew and Luke and also must have been greatly respected by them. Because of this, Mark can be considered to be more accurate historically.[12] Mark's gospel was accepted by the church at a time when eyewitnesses would still be in existence who would have challenged it if there had been any unwarranted elaboration of the events of Jesus' ministry. Thus, the gospel according to Mark is accorded a high respect because of its apparent priority and accuracy. The Markan hypothesis is built upon the assumption that the closer a document is to the events it records, the higher degree of authority and accuracy it has; the eyewitnesses will guarantee it.[13]

Source critics considered the Q document to be less important than the gospel of Mark. But the very nature of its contents, the

[11] For the details of the two-source hypothesis see Kümmel, *Introduction*. For an excellent survey of the current discussion of the alternatives to the two-source theory see Joseph A. Fitzmyer, S.J., 'The Priority of Mark and the "Q" Source in Luke', in *Jesus and Man's Hope*, I, (1970), pp. 131–70.

[12] H. J. Holtzmann provided the most definitive and persuasive statement of the Markan hypothesis in *Die synoptischen Evangelien: ihr Ursprung und geschichtlicher Charakter* (1863).

[13] For a contemporary emphasis on eyewitnesses see O. Cullmann, *Salvation in History* (1967), pp. 73, 98–102.

sayings of Jesus, would help to attest its accuracy. If we assume
that the early collectors were inherently honest, there is no reason
to suspect the basic accuracy of Q and therefore no reason to
suspect the authenticity of the sayings reported in it. The Semitic
quality of Q is also an indication of its early origin and therefore
its probable authenticity.[14]

The variations which exist between the synoptics are accounted
for by ascribing to Matthew and Luke a tendency to conflate or
expand the tradition in order to mould the ancient material into a
unified whole. This work is basically that of a collator who corrects
grammar and style to achieve a unified presentation, although he
is careful not to change the tone or message of the material he has
received. Matthew and Luke are considered collectors of tradition
rather than authors, editors rather than innovators.

Adolf Harnack and T. W. Manson are both source critics who
worked in two different eras yet reflected the concerns of source
criticism.

*Adolf Harnack*   Harnack wrote *The Sayings of Jesus* in 1906 in
response to Julius Wellhausen's *Einleitung in die drei ersten Evangelien*. Harnack assumes that a careful comparative study of Matthew
and Luke will enable him to recover the original text of Q. He
recognizes that Matthew and Luke have their own peculiar
characteristics and have obviously modified the original text.[15]
Because Luke is known to modify Mark in the interests of
smoother Greek, Harnack argues that Matthew's version of the
*demand* for a sign is the authentic one: '[They said,] Θέλομεν ἀπὸ
σοῦ σημεῖον ἰδεῖν'. The next sentence, the beginning of Jesus' reply,
is best preserved by Matthew also; Luke 'corrects' Q's more
barbarian Greek. Matthew's μοιχαλίς must also be original,
because it 'is elsewhere avoided by St Luke as a vulgar word'.[16]
With Matthew now recognized as preserving the more original
version of the incident, Harnack goes to the extreme of asserting
that Luke has replaced a compound verb (ἐπιζητεῖ) with the simple
ζητεῖ, even though Luke has a definite tendency to create com-
pounds: 'He appreciates the special meaning of the compound.'[17]

---

[14] See especially T. W. Manson, *The Sayings of Jesus* (1949; originally Part II
of H. D. A. Major, T. W. Manson and C. J. Wright, *The Mission and Message of
Jesus*, 1937).

[15] Harnack, *Sayings*, p. 23.    [16] *Ibid.*    [17] *Ibid.*

Thus, Harnack argues that Matthew is closer to the original word-ing of Q, in part because Harnack knows that Matthew is often closer to the wording of Mark and that Matthew would have a similar approach to the use of both Mark and Q.

However, when he comes to consider the explanation of the Sign of Jonah, Harnack argues that Luke's version is more authentic, except for Luke's replacing of ὥσπερ by καθώς. Matthew has interpreted Q and not copied it. We can be certain that Matthew's understanding of the Jonah comparison comes from Matthew because if it had existed in Q, Luke would certainly not have omitted it![18] Matthew has interpreted the Sign of Jonah as a reference to the descent into Hades. Since Luke is original, i.e. closer to Q, then the original saying must have been a reference to the preaching of Jonah: the sign which was given to the Ninevites. A prophet had come to Nineveh preaching repentance just as Jesus has come preaching repentance to this generation.

The double saying (Luke 11.31f. = Matt. 12.41f.), with the reversal of order in Matthew and Luke, must be explained on the basis of the sources. Harnack states that Matthew's order is original (Nineveh/Queen of the South), evidently because he has already shown that Matthew is closer to Q in the opening verses of the pericope. At any rate, he is not willing to ascribe the modifica-tion of the order of the double saying to the evangelist Luke. Rather, he suggests it might be explained as 'an ancient error of a scribe'; or even more likely, since Codex D omits Luke 11.32 (the Ninevite comparison) and since Luke 11.32 does not have the characteristic Lukan phrase, 'the men of this generation', as does Luke 11.31, the change in order is the result of an interpolation. Nevertheless, Harnack does not doubt that Matt. 12.41 and its parallel stood in the text of Q.[19]

Harnack does not go on to discuss the meaning of the text as he reconstructs it. He has assumed that behind the gospels of Matthew and Luke there stands a written document which has been copied, but which has not been followed exactly. He is very hesitant to ascribe any theologically motivated editorial activity to Matthew or Luke and instead seeks to ascribe variation, when possible, to the lapses of later scribes. Luke is the stylist and cor-rects the text in the interests of a smoother reading. But the disagreement in the explanation of the sign (Luke 11.30/Matt.

[18] *Ibid.*    [19] *Ibid.*, p. 24.

12.40) is so vast that Matthew must be held responsible for an interpretation of the sign that was not intended by Q.

Perhaps the most amazing aspect of Harnack's work is his apparent confidence in and easy acceptance of the reliability of the Q document. He evidently assumes that any early attempt to collect the sayings of Jesus was done under an impulse to preserve these statements because of their historic significance. The nineteenth-century historian would look with more respect upon those who collect material than upon those who attempt to tell the story of what was said and done. The collection of sayings is a much more legitimate approach toward an understanding of the historical Jesus. Thus, in his summary concerning the formal characteristics of Q, Harnack asserts that the Q document is 'without any clearly discernible bias, whether apologetic, didactic, ecclesiastical, national or anti-national'.[20]

*T. W. Manson*  Manson represents a later stage in the source-critical analysis of the gospels. *The Sayings of Jesus* was first published in 1937, and yet Manson demonstrates many of the same nuances at work in his analysis of the Q material as we have found in Harnack. His confidence in the authenticity of the Q sayings is just as strong: 'The largest part of the tradition must, however, be credited to the disciples.'[21] The eyewitness character of the material and its subsequent circulation among eyewitnesses demands that we give full attention to the sayings as sources for the very words of Jesus. Manson even states that this early group of sayings is arranged chronologically; connected sayings were spoken on the same occasion or on successive occasions.[22]

A basic change in orientation from Harnack is evident when we note that Manson has widened his concern to include Mark. Harnack had a very narrow view of the extent of intersynoptic influence. Q, to him, was a document which had been used by Matthew and Luke, as they had used Mark. The authors of Matthew and Luke would not have confused one document with the other; they were collectors of the tradition which had been handed down in documentary form. Manson, on the other hand has a view of the responsibility of Matthew and Luke which allows more freedom in the manipulation of the tradition. He has recognized that Luke is more restrained in modifying his sources, except for stylistic changes, and that Matthew has apparently been much freer in rearranging his material. Thus, Manson tends to find Luke closer to the Q source both in details of content and in its arrangement.[23] Much of Manson's analysis presupposes this understanding of the order of Q, an order based primarily on Luke's Gospel.

Manson's respect for Luke as a source in reconstructing Q is evident at the very beginning of his work. Matthew, Mark and Luke disagree about the identity of those who demand a sign. Manson decides that Matthew and Mark have good reason to be specific and that Luke's general reference to 'others' is probably closer to Q;[24] this, despite the fact that Luke has separated the demand (11.16) from the reply (11.29f.). Luke 11.29 would today be considered an obvious editorial introduction and therefore Lukan; not so for Manson. The influence of the theological point of view is, however, admitted when Manson ascribes the deletion of μοιχαλίς in Luke to its probable meaninglessness in a Gentile environment.[25] (Cf. Harnack: Luke would not have used such a vulgar word.) The possibility that Matthew may have added it, though, is not considered by Manson because of his view of the nature of the work being done by Matthew; Matthew records eye-witness accounts and is thereby an editor with a historical interest in accuracy.

Manson agrees with Harnack that the explanation in Luke 11.30 is from Q and that Matt. 12.40 must be the work of Matthew, who is attempting to clarify the meaning of an enigmatic statement. Luke 11.30 is not only Q, then, but also the authentic word of Jesus. The problem for Manson is to explain why Matthew would have used a quotation from the Septuagint which does not exactly correspond to the facts of the death and resurrection; Jesus was not in the grave three days and three nights. He suggests that it is typical of Matthew to modify facts to serve his purpose, and therefore we must assume that the discrepancy was not a problem for him; that Matthew may have 'thought that his account was near enough to the facts'.[26]

Manson's great confidence in the authenticity and accuracy of the sources becomes clear when he responds to the suggestion that Luke 11.30 and Matt. 12.40 may both be 'glosses' or later additions. This is not possible, says Manson, because we could only call them

[23] *Ibid.,* p. 89.    [24] *Ibid.*    [25] *Ibid.,* p. 89.    [26] *Ibid.,* p. 90.

glosses if their meaning was such 'that it could not reasonably be supposed to be the thought of Jesus'.[27] The tradition is authentic until proven otherwise. His assumption is that any development would be away from any semblance of similarity to the known words of Jesus. Since this saying, especially Luke 11.30, does 'reasonably' make sense in relation to other sayings of Jesus, we must reject any suggestion of inauthenticity.[28]

The same basic source-critical assumption stands out in Manson's comment on the suggestion that Jonah is a mistranslation for John.[29] If this were the case, one would have to ascribe the explanations (Luke 11.30 = Matt. 12.40) to Matthew and Luke themselves and, in effect, claim that they were glosses, i.e. not from the original sources and therefore not authentic. Manson's comment is quite simple: 'Against this solution is the fact that it would deprive the ministry of Jesus of significance.'[30]

Since Matthew has shown his freedom to change the tradition by trying to explain a difficult passage with the insertion of a quotation from Jonah 2.1, Manson can also ascribe to Matthew the reordering of the double saying; this rearrangement was necessary because Matthew must bring the Jonah and Ninevite saying (12.41) into close proximity to the revised explanation (12.40). Luke's order is chronological and probably preserves the order of Q.[31]

What then does the reconstructed Q saying mean? Manson argues that since the opponents of Jesus wanted some authentication of his messiahship, Jesus is merely denying them this kind of sign. Jonah preached and was heard; the same response should be the reaction of this generation. Q and Mark say the same thing: No sign will be given. The authentication is the message.

## Word Study and Jewish Background

The understanding of the New Testament which is inherent in the *Theologisches Wörterbuch zum Neuen Testament* demands con-

---

[27] *Ibid.*      [28] *Ibid.*

[29] C. Moxon, 'τὸ σημεῖον 'Ιωνᾶ', *ExpT* XXII (1911), 566f; J. H. Michael, 'The Sign of John', *JTS* XXI (1920), 146–59; cf. also Dom John Howton, 'The Sign of Jonah', *SJT* XV (1962), pp. 288–304, in which Jonah is considered a transliteration of the Aramaic word for dove.

[30] Manson, *Sayings*, p. 90.

[31] *Ibid.*, p. 91.

sideration as a distinctive method of gospel study. The contributors to that dictionary assume, to a greater or lesser degree, that a study of the use of a particular word in biblical and non-biblical material will enable us to gain some insight into the working of the Hebrew and/or biblical writer's mind. In relation to the Sign of Jonah, it is assumed that once we have surveyed the understanding of Jonah which existed in the first century, we shall then be able to imagine what some of those who heard the saying might have thought it meant. If we can locate the ways in which 'sign' is used at this time, we may gain some insight into how Jesus' hearers might have understood the request.

There are two articles in the *TWNT* which are relevant, to an investigation of the Sign of Jonah – the article *"Ἰωνᾶς"* by Joachim Jeremias[32] and the article *'σημεῖον'* written by Karl Rengstorf.[33]

*Joachim Jeremias*   Jeremias argues that the Sign of Jonah saying was originally a riddle to those who heard it. In this sense, Mark 8.11f., Luke 11.30 and Matt. 12.40 are really making the same point. Jesus' reply took the form of the saying in Luke 11.30 and means: the point of comparison between Jonah and Jesus is the deliverance from death. Matt. 12.40 is a later interpretation which quotes Jonah 2.1 literally and modifies the original comparison by shifting the application to the short time spent in Sheol from the fact of the deliverance. The Son of Man returning from the dead will be the only sign – obviously not the kind of sign which is requested. 'Both statements (Luke 11.30 and Mark 8.12) make it clear that God will not give any sign that is abstracted from the person of Jesus and that does not give offence.'[34]

Thus Jeremias places the weight of his interpretation on the fish incident and not on the preaching of repentance in Nineveh. Luke 11.30 and Matt. 12.40 both stress the significance of Jesus' resurrection from the dead by a comparison with Jonah's deliverance from the gates of *Sheol*. Jeremias is led to this conclusion by a survey of the significance ascribed to Jonah in 'late Judaism'. This survey of the mention of Jonah in Jewish material makes clear that it was the fish incident which attracted more attention than Jonah's preaching ministry. A Jonah-type deliverance from sea

[32] Joachim Jeremias, *"Ἰωνᾶς"*, *TDNT* III, 406–10.
[33] Karl Rengstorf, *'σημεῖον'*, *TWNT* VII, 199–261.
[34] Jeremias, *"Ἰωνᾶς"*, p. 410.

monsters and from the chaos of the sea is a universal religious theme, as the historians of religion have shown.[35] Almost all the legends which surround Jonah in Jewish literature concentrate on the first two chapters of the book. At the same time, Jeremias points out, Jonah is vindicated as a righteous prophet; his flight was necessary to avoid bringing judgment upon Israel; he sacrificed himself to save those on the ship (Jonah 1.12). Thus there can be little doubt, according to Jeremias, that in the contemporary environment, the mention of Jonah would probably evoke some image related to his salvation from the fish.

Jeremias notes further that there are three possible ways to understand the genitive case in the phrase τὸ σημεῖον ᾽Ιωνᾶ: (1) appositive genitive (the sign which was given in the prophet Jonah), (2) subjective genitive (the sign which Jonah gave), (3), objective genitive (the sign which Jonah experienced). The grammatical problem cannot be solved prior to an interpretation of the saying as a whole.[36]

Jeremias offers three of the most significant interpretations, all of which are rejected by him.

1. The misreading of ᾽Ιωνᾶ for ᾽Ιωάν(ν)ης rests on insecure linguistic grounds.
2. The sign as Jesus' present preaching is ruled out because of the future verb ἔσται in Luke 11.30 and Matt. 12.40.
3. Matthew's use of the time element as the point of comparison is rejected as obviously secondary, as a shift away from the deliverance theme which is so evident in Luke.

Jeremias' interpretation is based on the assumption that part of Jonah's message to the Ninevites was the story of his miraculous deliverance from death.

A further assumption behind Jeremias' solution is also clear. He has assumed that Jesus would speak in a way which would be comprehensible to his hearers. A reference to Jonah would bring to the hearer's mind a picture of Jonah and his salvation from the fish, i.e. a deliverance from *Sheol* and death. Because he can find little contemporary interest in Jonah as a preacher, the fish incident becomes the basis of interpretation. Although Jeremias has a

---

[35] Uwe Steffen, *Das Mysterium Von Tod und Auferstehung: Formen und Wandlungen des Jona-Motive* (1963).
[36] Jeremias, "᾽Ιωνᾶ", p. 408.

greater interest in the extent of, and motives for, the editorial work of the evangelists, especially in the case of Matthew, he is primarily interested in recovering the words of Jesus, and therefore seeks to recreate the 'environment' so that we might also listen as Jesus' first hearers listened. Interest in the authenticity of the sources and their genuine cultural accuracy is especially clear when Jeremias comments: Jesus is using a 'mashal form, so that only initiates see that He is speaking of Himself'.[37]

*Karl Rengstorf*   Rengstorf's article on σημεῖον is more typical of the *TWNT* approach. Having much more material to work with, he surveys the Jewish and Greek literature, seeking a distinctive usage in either tradition. Rengstorf discovers that although certain specific usages can be found, none becomes predominant and no specific pattern exists which would assist in defining the use of 'sign' in the Jonah material; each case must be decided on its own merits and in terms of its own peculiarity. Therefore, when dealing with the Sign of Jonah, the most that can be said in this context is that there is good Old Testament precedent for referring to a man as a sign (e.g. Isa. 8.18; 20.3; Ezek. 12.6).[38] Rengstorf likewise points to the midrashic references to Jonah which speak of what God accomplished through Jonah. We are justified, he says, in accepting the genitive construction as one of apposition; the sign of Jonah is the sign which was given in the prophet Jonah.

What is it that was given in Jonah? Most likely, Rengstorf says, the 'particularity of his historical appearance'.[39] The preaching of Jonah is compared to the preaching of Jesus; God acts in the prophet through the effectiveness of his call for repentance. Jonah represents the effectiveness of God. Jonah, as a person, is not the point of comparison.

Thus Rengstorf accepts the Lukan version of the explanation as the probable form of Q and rejects Matt. 12.40 as late and secondary. The nature of his assumptions becomes clear when he criticizes Jeremias for finding the sign in the 'preaching of repentance done by Jonah'.[40] This interpretation goes beyond the bounds of the possible meaning of the word 'sign'; it can refer to a person, but not to the preaching activity in particular. But

---

[37] *Ibid.*, p. 410 n. 29.    [38] Rengstorf, 'σημεῖον', p. 232.
[39] *Ibid.*, p. 231.    [40] *Ibid.*, p. 232.

Rengstorf refuses to go beyond this judgment to solve the particular 'riddle-like' character of the saying.[41]

The limitations of this method are now clear. It is certainly useful to know how a word is used, or how a person is described, but this information cannot solve the problem of any given text. It can offer a limit of meaning, as Rengstorf's criticism of Jeremias illustrates, but it will not offer a solution within the limits set, without relying on other means to clarify the text. Rengstorf shows more reticence then Jeremias in achieving some answer to the question of what Jesus actually said, even though he does hope to find some help by a survey of the use of the word 'sign'.

The results of this method are meagre and demand that some other avenue of approach be explored if we are to achieve any real solution.

## Form Criticism

Form criticism is built upon the assumption that there lies behind the written sources of the gospels a developed and complex oral tradition. In a period of oral transmission the material will take on specific formal or structural characteristics which will reflect the situation in which that material is used. The form critic then is one who is seeking to move behind written documents to the small independent units of tradition which, when isolated, will enable him to discover not only the situation in which this unit was preserved but also to trace the variation of application in its transmission; that is, he hopes to be able to write a history of the tradition. In its early stages, form criticism was engaged in the task of classifying small units of tradition and tracing them back from the written form, through successive layers of modification, to the earliest material. It was assumed that the purer or more simple the form, the greater the likelihood of its antiquity.[42]

With these principles in operation, it is not surprising to discover that form critics have not been very interested in the Sign of Jonah passages. It is only too obvious to them that this is a situation where later editors, probably Matthew and Luke, have been at work in attempting to clarify a confusing reference in the

[41] *Ibid.*

[42] Rudolf Bultmann, *The History of the Synoptic Tradition*, trans. from 3rd German ed. (1963); Martin Dibelius, *From Tradition to Gospel*, trans. from 2nd German ed. (1935).

earlier tradition. When compared with Mark, it may be that the entire Jonah reference is secondary. Thus attention is directed to Mark 8.11–13, to the refusal to give any sign, as well as to the double saying (Luke 11.31f.=Matt. 12.41f.) which by itself has certain Jewish characteristics and may be very early. V. Taylor illustrates the difficulty form critics have in coming to some agreement even about the form of the Markan refusal-saying. He says, 'It may be a pronouncement story, but is perhaps more probably a Story about Jesus constructed by the Evangelist himself.'[43] At any rate, the Sign of Jonah complex of passages has not been a major concern for form critics.

*Rudolf Bultmann*   Bultmann in *The History of the Synoptic Tradition* is primarily interested in showing the obvious secondary character of Matthew's interpretation of the sign of Jonah. He classifies this pericope as a 'Minatory Saying', part of the larger category of 'Prophetic and Apocalyptic Sayings'.[44] It is obvious to Bultmann that Luke's vagueness of definition (11.30) indicates the earlier origin of the saying, since the tendency of the tradition is to expand, elaborate and fill in the gaps. Luke seems to refer to the heavenly origin of the Son of Man and not to his death and resurrection. Bultmann suggests that the original meaning based on Luke 11.30 was probably a comparison of the coming of the heavenly Son of Man with Jonah's appearance at Nineveh from a foreign land.[45]

The origin of the Jonah comparison is difficult to determine, says Bultmann. Some have suggested that it is a creation of the Q tradition, but it is also possible that Mark has omitted the reference to Jonah because it was incomprehensible to him. The latter explanation seems more likely to Bultmann.[46]

Of more interest to Bultmann is the double saying from Q. In this comparison-saying, Jewish material has been taken over by the early community and ascribed to Jesus. Matt. 11.21–24 is another example of a similar form. The original order would most likely have been chronological (Solomon before Jonah) in an independent saying; the reversal of the order must be Matthew's work, necessitated by his elaboration of the explanation. Thus Bultmann claims that the church has taken over two prophetic

[43] Vincent Taylor, *The Gospel According to St Mark,* (2nd ed. 1966), p. 361.
[44] Bultmann, *History*, p. 112.    [45] *Ibid.*, p. 118.    [46] *Ibid.*

warnings and applied them to the present – a typical tendency of
Q. The warning contained in the double saying is brought to-
gether with the Sign of Jonah, probably because the name of
Jonah occurs in each.[47]

The result of Bultmann's analysis: the earliest level of tradition
is the refusal to give a sign; early in the history of the church an
exception is attached, 'except the sign of Jonah'; the warning
(double saying) is added to the refusal in the Q tradition, most
likely because of the catchword Jonah. Luke may represent an
early explanation, but Matthew is certainly late.

*Martin Dibelius*   Dibelius is even less interested in the Sign of
Jonah.[48] He lists Mark 8.11–13 as one of four examples within the
Gospels where minimal data is supplied to clarify the situation in
which a saying of Jesus was pronounced. Although the saying
does not stand by itself, it comes as close as any other to the stark
simplicity of the Greek *chriae*.[49] To Dibelius, this would indicate
a later stage in the tradition when Greek forms of speech exert
some influence on the form of the gospel sayings.

Form-critical neglect of the Sign of Jonah is a natural outcome
of the method. By discarding later additions the early material, and
hence the more significant evidence, can be isolated. The many
indications of redaction in these four passages have required that
the form critic look elsewhere for the earliest material. But form
critics have become increasingly aware of the fact that even the
earliest levels of tradition were preserved by the church because of
their relevance to its work and not because of a strictly historical,
chronicle-like interest; we must be more aware of the impact of
the thoughts and purposes of those who preserve and establish all
tradition.

After the Second World War, form criticism began to turn its
attention toward that material which it had previously set aside,
the redactional additions or framework. Redaction criticism attempts to assess the theological intention of each level of tradition
which form criticism has uncovered.

*Redaction Criticism*

Redaction criticism might be called framework criticism because
it is an attempt to evaluate what the form critics called 'the frame-

[47] *Ibid.*, p. 112.    [48] Dibelius, *Tradition*.    [49] *Ibid.*, pp. 159f.

work', the material which the editor or redactor had created to contain the units of tradition which he received.[50] It is built upon the assumption that the intention of the redactor is apparent in the way in which he modifies and arranges the material he receives. Assuming the two-document hypothesis, the editorial activity of Matthew and Luke is quite apparent when we see the specific alterations they have made in the wording and arrangement of Mark. When the character of the sources or earlier tradition is less certain, the redaction critic must focus his attention more completely on the composition or the structure of the Gospel. Thus, Ernst Haenchen has suggested that redaction criticism might be called 'Komposition' criticism.[51] The unifying factor in all this work is the search for the so-called 'third *Sitz im Leben*', the *Sitz im Leben der Evangelist*. Form criticism had already distinguished between the *Sitz im Leben Jesu* and the *Sitz im Leben der alten Kirche*. The third *Sitz* is the theological *Sitz im Leben* because redaction criticism assumes that the theological stance of the redactor will make itself known in all aspects of his work.[52] The evangelists and their predecessors are evaluated no longer as mere collectors or assemblers of units of tradition, but rather they are respected as theologians in their own right, men who indicate their understanding of the received tradition by the way in which it is recorded.

Clearly, then, redaction criticism is a development of form criticism and cannot operate without form-critical presuppositions. At the same time, it represents a new approach to the New Testament by shifting the focus of attention from the recovery of the earliest material to the richness and creativity of the church's development of its traditions. If there is a history of the tradition, as form criticism had shown, why concentrate only on the earliest levels, especially when they too appear to be under the creative influence of the community? Redaction criticism has demanded that New Testament critics move from a concern for the small primary units of tradition to the larger more complex collections represented by the gospels and earlier compositions. Hans Conzelmann has called the programme of redaction criticism an

[50] For a general description of redaction criticism see Joachim Rohde, *Rediscovering the Teaching of the Evangelists* (1968).

[51] Ernst Haenchen, *Der Weg Jesu: Eine Erklärung des Markus-Evangeliums und der kanonischen Parallelen* (1966), p. 24.

[52] Rohde, *Rediscovering*, pp. 9–30.

attempt to deal with a second phase in the development of Christianity, when the kerygma is not simply transmitted but itself becomes the subject of reflection.[53]

The primary assumption of redaction criticism is its acceptance of the freedom and independence of the redactor. The New Testament is viewed as a pre-Enlightenment document which is primarily an expression of the faith of the early church, at various times and places, and reflected in different levels of the tradition. A related assumption states that the theological stance of each redactor will be reflected in his redaction; rather than collectors, we can begin to talk about creative editors.[54]

*Heinz Eduard Tödt*   The primary example of a redaction-critical understanding of the Sign of Jonah is the work of H. E. Tödt.[55] His interest is, of course, the Son of Man reference in the explanation (Luke 11.30 and Matt. 12.40) as well as the fact that this material shows signs of coming from the Q community. Rather than searching for the words of Jesus, or the possible earliest tradition, his concern is with each level of redaction and its understanding of the Son of Man. Tödt is hindered by a prior assumption that the Sayings about the future Son of Man are authentic, and he does not consistently make full use of the method he has chosen.[56] None the less, a close look merely at the Table of Contents in his book will show that this is definitely an essay in redaction criticism.

Tödt's reconstruction of the history of the tradition starts from the claim that the Q stratum contained the phrase 'except the sign of Jonah' to supplement a saying refusing a sign, as well as a following explanation 'stating some kind of analogy between the Son of Man and Jonah'.[57] Luke 11.30 is most likely the Q version of the explanation; Matthew's quotation is late.

The double saying makes a different point when it refers to Jonah; Jesus is said to be greater than Jonah. This fact, plus the change in the order of the double saying in Matthew, leads Tödt to conclude that the double saying originally existed as a separate unit and was attached to Luke 11.30 because of a common reference to Jonah.[58]

---

[53] Hans Conzelmann, *The Theology of St Luke* (1961), p. 12.
[54] Cf. Perrin, *Rediscovering*, ch. I.
[55] Heinz E. Tödt, *The Son of Man in the Synoptic Tradition* (1965).
[56] *Op. cit.*, esp. pp. 64–7.   [57] *Ibid.*, p. 211.   [58] *Ibid.*, p. 212.

When Luke received this tradition from Q, he saw no reason to expand or modify it. The demand for a sign indicates that 'this evil generation' is truly evil. The only sign is Jesus' own teaching, which is not the kind of sign demanded, but it is the sign which the Ninevites received and to which they responded. By refusing to repent at the preaching of Jesus, this generation will be judged. Tödt has made Luke 11.30 equivalent to 11.32 even though he sees them as originally independent. It is the authority of Jesus which Q is emphasizing and Luke continues this emphasis. The future Son of Man will confirm the authority which Jesus commands.[59]

Matthew, therefore, has moved in a direction not intended by the original saying. Tödt suggests that once the establishment of a close connection between 'rising after three days' and the 'Son of Man' has occurred, it would not be difficult to see the point of comparison in the time spent in the realm of death rather than in the preaching. Tödt had already established that the suffering Son of Man tradition is a later phenomenon which first appears in Mark, and that Matthew is combining two traditions in his explanation. Matthew sees Jonah as the type of the suffering Son of Man, not of the judging, future Son of Man.[60]

It is in Q that we must seek an answer to the question of the meaning of the Sign of Jonah. Tödt's analysis of the theological stance of Q shows that Jesus is considered to be the authoritative teacher who summons men to follow him. Attention is focused on Jesus' presence and on the impact coming within the present situation. 'The future is determined by the effect of his presence.'[61] Thus the theology of Q can point us in the right direction if we wish to uncover the meaning of the Sign of Jonah saying. Jeremias' interpretation of the sign is rejected by Tödt precisely in this way. Since the death and resurrection theme is not part of Q's programme, to claim that the reference to Jonah stresses that the one who is sent by God is legitimized by being rescued from death, is to import a later, or at least variant, theological tradition into the Q material. 'This would be the only case of a saying from Q speaking in anticipation of the Son of Man's rising.'[62]

Thus, Tödt's history of the tradition would begin with a statement by Jesus equivalent to Luke 11.30. This Jonah-saying is later added to a double saying because of the mention of Jonah in each. Matthew has expanded one element of the original saying at a

[59] *Ibid.*, p. 53.   [60] *Ibid.*, p. 212.   [61] *Ibid.*, p. 266.   [62] *Ibid.*, p. 212.

later time, while Luke takes over the Q material almost intact. Tödt does not attempt to explain the relation of Mark 8.11–13 to the Q saying.

## Solution Proposed by Anton Vögtle

The most important recent attempt to solve the Sign of Jonah problem is the article by Anton Vögtle. We turn now to his constructive suggestions.

The survey of the recent research led Vögtle to the judgment that Luke 11.30 is closer to the *Vorlage* than Matt. 12.40. He hoped to clarify the problem by assuming that if Luke 11.29 was authentic it could not have been completely incomprehensible to Jesus' audience, although it may have been riddle-like. A mere reference to the Sign of Jonah is not concrete enough to be immediately clear to everyone, if it is indeed clear to anyone. However, after Easter and Pentecost, the parousia is recognized as the promised guarantee which will convince the unbelieving generation; the parousia will be a messianic authentication. Vögtle points to Mark 14.62 as an example of the way in which the Son of Man concept and the parousia are related. The parousia could be a direct authentication of the messianic claims made by Jesus. The resurrection, argues Vögtle, would be essential kerygmatic material which would point ahead to the parousia, the actual event of authentication; the death and resurrection are presuppositions of the completion soon to come. What is riddle-like must be explained and the statement of Christ must be clarified – not only for missionary purposes, but also for christological purposes, i.e. that Christ spoke of himself as the Sign of Jonah. The church, then, uses the title Son of Man as a way of building up an explanation of the Sign of Jonah and Jesus speaks in a manner similar to that of the prophets. The title Son of Man can serve two purposes: either as a reference to the death and resurrection or as a reference to the future parousia. Vögtle is hesitant about asserting that Jesus may have spoken about a suffering Son of Man, but he says there is no doubt that Jesus did use Son of Man to refer to his parousia. Thus 11.29 suggests the possibility of 11.30.

The creation of 11.30 by the church is not immediate, says Vögtle, for he suggests that the earliest explanation would be similar to: 'the Son of Man will be a sign to this generation'.[63] The verb ἔσται is used in contrast to the passive δοθήσεται in 11.29. Thus a type of parable is formed – the history of Jonah indicates how the Son of Man will be a sign to this generation. This parable would suggest a comparison statement which would relate the wonder of Jonah to the wonder of the Son of Man: as Jonah, so also the Son of Man. However, at this stage 'to the Ninevites' is added to parallel the fact that the Son of Man is a sign 'to this generation'. Now a problem has arisen: Jonah's resurrection is not an authenticating wonder experienced by the Ninevites. Thus a kerygmatic statement has been developed which clouds the issue and thereby reveals its secondary origin. Since 11.29 does not mention Nineveh, and because the problem is overcome by seeing 11.30 developed in this way, we are left with the result: Luke 11.30 is a kerygmatic expansion of the original riddle-like saying.[64]

In his summary (Part Six), Vögtle points to the 'living adaptation and creativity' which is part of the formation of the gospel narratives.[65] Mark can easily be understood as having recognized in Jesus' answer a simple 'no', and he therefore clarifies it by deleting the mention of the Sign of Jonah. Nor is the explanation of Luke 11.30 a falsification or invention, instead, it is a part of the proclamation of the Son of Man. Matt. 12.40 is not just a reference to the resurrection, because Matthew knows that the Jews have not responded to it as a sign of authentication. Matthew concentrates on the specifics of the *Sign* of Jonah and quotes Jonah 2.1, but his intent is to point ahead to the parousia: the resurrection is the anticipation of the parousia. Matthew has merely combined the idea of the Sign of the Son of Man (Matt. 24.30) with the Sign of Jonah; the Son of Man is risen, it is he who will come. Thus the two events are really part of the same reality.[66]

## Response to Vögtle

Vögtle's work is clearly based upon the principles of tradition history, or more generally, form criticism. Any criticism of his work must either challenge him for using an improper method to deal with this material or must point out mistakes and bad judgments, or improper implementation of the approved method. It is the first of these alternatives which seems more important because Vögtle has not seen the implication of the form-critical method

[63] 'Jonaszeichen', p. 272.    [64] *Ibid.*, pp. 272f.    [65] *Ibid.*, pp. 273–7.
[66] *Ibid.*, pp. 276f.

which has brought redaction criticism into the foreground of gospel study. If Vögtle had supplemented his analysis of the traditions with an overall view of the purpose of each level of the tradition, his conclusions about the development of the 'kerygmatic explanation' would have been grounded on a firmer foundation. As it is, he has suggested a very plausible solution, but has no way to control or demonstrate its probability. In a certain sense he is anticipating redaction criticism, as many form critics did, by showing that there *was* development within these so-called primitive traditions, developments which go back much farther than had been anticipated. If there was this kerygmatic freedom, then each tradition should represent a relatively unified stage and would, as a unity, offer more insight into the actual progress or movement of the change that has obviously occurred.

When Vögtle isolates Luke 11.30 as the earliest stratum of the explanation, as Q, he fails to ask about the character of Q and the theological leanings which would have led to the development of this form of the saying (Luke 11.30). He has done something similar with Matthew, to a limited extent, but apparently does not want to question either the authenticity of Luke 11.29 (even though it is clearly different from Mark) *or* to raise the basic question of the actual authenticity of the pericope as a whole. Nor is the question of a possible *Sitz im Leben* ever raised. Thus Vögtle's work seems incomplete and therefore, finally, inadequate.

Is it possible to arrive at a general, multi-level conclusion about the meaning of the word 'sign', as Vögtle does? Could it be that a variety of meanings have been placed on this word and therefore a variety of explanations and decisions about the meaning of the entire phrase, 'except the sign of Jonah'? If there are possible variations, then the specific meaning implied by each level of the tradition must be carefully sought out by a study of each level.

The details of a redaction-critical analysis will be illustrated in chapter III of this book. But in order to implement this modification of method, it will be necessary first to indicate the style of theology which seems to be characteristic of each level of tradition. And because the Q material is so crucial to an analysis of the Sign of Jonah, we must be as precise as possible about the interests of that community. Then, in chapter III, we will be in a position to examine closely the history of the tradition of the Sign of Jonah saying, supplemented by the added insights of redaction criticism.

# II

## REDACTION CRITICISM OF THE
## GOSPELS AND Q

### THE THEOLOGY OF THE EVANGELISTS

As STATED at the end of chapter I, this section of the book is designed to set the limits of the redaction-critical approach to the Sign of Jonah. Redaction criticism is a method which is basically synthetic, in that it must deal with a wide range of material to find the pattern and character of the work of the final redactor. If we are to use this method in dealing with the Sign of Jonah, it will be necessary to report on the limited amount of work already completed on the gospels as a whole in order to supply a context in which to consider a small unit, such as the Sign of Jonah. With the basic orientation thus sketched, we can propose a solution to the more detailed problems at hand. This survey will also offer further insight into the application of the method.

Although the three synoptic gospels have been under redactional consideration for some time, the Q material has not received any extensive treatment beyond the work done by H. E. Tödt. Since this level of the tradition will be of special concern to us in chapter III, it is necessary to go into more detail in dealing with Q than with the three gospels.

### Mark

Any statement of Mark's theology must begin with a recognition of Dibelius' epigram: Mark is 'a book of secret epiphanies'.[1] It is the elaboration of this statement which supplies the details of the Markan theology. Marxsen has called Mark the great theologian of the cross, the one who 'worked backwards' in creating the form

---

[1] Dibelius, *Tradition,* p. 230.

'gospel' by arranging everything in terms of the redemptive suffering and death of Jesus, the Son of God.[2]

Marxsen's redaction study of Mark was also a programmatic essay in redaction criticism. And although many scholars would not agree with the historical dimension of Marxsen's hypothesis (that Mark was written in Galilee between AD 66 and 69),[3] most would acknowledge that Mark stands at an early point in the church's attempt to cope with the problem of the delay of the parousia.[4] We must give some credit to those who insist that the very recording of the church's message points in that direction.[5] Nevertheless, Mark has no developed concept of the church and has not attempted to elaborate the problems of the extended wait for the end. His concern is more immediate: to present the message of the church and thereby to combat specific misunderstandings about the person of Jesus. That is to say, Mark's gospel is primarily a statement of christology. The fact that it is presented as a narrative is part of the creativity which Mark or his community has brought to the completion of this task.[6]

It is primarily the outline or structure of the gospel which has been the clue to the character of Mark's gospel. Most of the material which Mark uses seems to have been handed down to him from the tradition before him; his contribution is in using these varied traditions in a dynamic way, to theologize by the use of the narrative form. Conzelmann places Mark between the oral tradition and the written gospels of Matthew and Luke. This is an early stage in the reflection upon the material and not just a matter of simple transference of stable, written documents.[7]

One of Mark's more important editorial characteristics is the theological use to which he puts geography.[8] The gospel is divided into two major epochs, Galilee and the journey to Jeru-

[2] Willi Marxsen, *Der Evangelist Markus: Studien zur Redaktionsgeschichte des Evangeliums* (2nd ed., 1959). Cf. also Heinz-Dieter Knigge, 'The Meaning of Mark: The exegesis of the second Gospel', *Interpretation* XXII (1968), pp. 53–70.

[3] Marxsen, *Markus,* p. 70.

[4] Hans Conzelmann, *An Outline of the Theology of the New Testament* (1969), pp. 140–4, and the bibliography.

[5] Conzelmann, *Outline,* p. 141 and n. 4.

[6] Norman Perrin, 'The Son of Man in the Synoptic Tradition' (unpublished paper presented at the annual meeting of the Society of Biblical Literature in New York on 27 Dec. 1967), pp. 22–8 (mimeographed).

[7] Conzelmann, *Outline,* p. 142.

[8] Conzelmann, *ibid.,* pp. 142–4, and Marxsen, *Markus,* pp. 18, 19, 141f.

salem. It is in Galilee that Jesus performs wonders and presents in basic outline the message he proclaims; it is on the journey to Jerusalem that the true character of the message is revealed. It is impossible to differentiate the secrecy motif from the geographical references. The movement toward Jerusalem begins when the disciples begin to understand the real nature of the messiahship Jesus has announced.

After the work done in Galilee, Jesus retreats to the north, beyond Galilee, and the major turning point occurs at Caesarea Philippi where the first indications of the true character of the Messiah are announced, the suffering of the Son of Man (Mark 8.27ff.). Yet the insight of Peter, as a representative of the disciples, is still deficient, and the plot moves toward Jerusalem where the 'predictions' are fulfilled. It is in the passion story that the real revelation takes place. 'Peter's confession and the transfiguration usher in the period of the passion, rather than that of open messianic proclamation.'[9] The secrecy motive is Mark's literary device to explain the inability of the disciples to come to a full realization of Jesus in his earthly life.[10]

In chs. 8, 9 and 10 Mark presents three separate statements of the suffering which is necessary for the one designated as Messiah. Each time the prediction is followed by some misunderstanding and finally by some teaching about discipleship.[11]

The time spent in Jerusalem is compressed into a few days and the crisis is quickly reached. Jerusalem is the place where the forces of evil triumph and the return of Jesus is scheduled for Galilee (16.7) – the land of proclamation. The judgment of ch. 13 upon Jerusalem is thus fulfilled in the narration of events.

Conzelmann has noted that in a very specific sense Mark's gospel is merely a commentary on the kerygma: Acts 2.22–24 asserts, first, that God has shown wonders through Jesus and, secondly, that Jesus was crucified and raised according to God's plan.[12] Thus a twofold statement of the kerygma does seem to exist prior to Mark and could have supplied the outline of his work.

[9] Conzelmann, *Outline*, p. 142.
[10] William Wrede, *Das Messiasgeheimnis in den Evangelien. Zugleich ein Beitrag zum Verstandnis des Markusevangeliums* (1901). Cf. also Knigge, 'Mark', for a report on the response to Wrede.
[11] Norman Perrin, *What is Redaction Criticism?* (1969).
[12] Conzelmann, *Outline*, p. 143.

Recent analysis of the titles in Mark has reinforced the judgment that Mark's purpose is christological.[13] It is argued that Mark is combating a false Son-of-God christology by placing a false christology on the lips of the demons and the disciples, while Jesus is portrayed as the one who constantly corrects this view as he prepares them for the actual drama of the passion. The messianic secret is part of Mark's explanation of the failure of the disciples to respond to the passion in the way expected. The gospel begins (1.1) and ends (15.39) with confessional statements about Jesus as the Son of God, and both statements indicate that the gospel is contained in the life and words of Jesus. The centurion acknowledges Jesus as the Son of God when he has just witnessed the *death* of Jesus, before the resurrection has taken place!

As Jesus establishes his authority as Son of Man acting in the present, he constantly demands silence of those exorcized demons who recognize him, while at the same time, men remain blind (cf. the Beelzebub controversy). But when recognition does occur on the part of the disciples at Caesarea Philippi, Jesus immediately redefines messiahship in terms of the suffering Son of Man. This teaching and its implications are repeated twice more (9.31ff.; 10.33ff.). Finally, Mark 10.45 functions as a summary of the passion which is about to begin; the suffering of Jesus is redemptive, not merely part of the mystery of God's ways. Mark does use some future Son of Man sayings (13.26; 14.62, etc.), but he does not allow the suffering theme to be sidetracked. The apocalyptic element is relegated to a secondary position while the death and resurrection occupies the primary position. The Son of Man material, of three basic types, has been interwoven by Mark; his technique is to arrange and order the tradition rather than rewrite it. Thus, the centurion's statement at the cross sums up the redefined christology: Jesus is the Son of God who suffers for the redemption of many.[14]

Given this basic understanding of Mark there are certain special themes which are of interest to us.

[13] T. J. Weeden, 'The Heresy that Necessitated Mark's Gospel' (unpublished dissertation at Claremont Graduate School, Claremont, California, 1967). Vernon Robbins, 'The Christology of Mark' (unpublished dissertation presented to the Divinity School, University of Chicago, 1969).
[14] Perrin, *Redaction Criticism*, pp. 51–57. Robbins, 'Mark'.

First, the emphasis on temptation has been noted by some scholars as offering a key to Mark's understanding of the cross. Ernest Best has argued that the brief account of the temptation in Mark 1.12f. demonstrates that Satan is bound for the duration of the ministry of Jesus and that, when temptation reappears, it is presented strictly as a human threat or demand.[15] In contrast to J. M. Robinson,[16] Best would assert that the death and suffering of Jesus is caused by the evil of man and is not the result of a cosmic attack by the forces of evil. When Jesus is tempted, it is the work of men who are trying to deflect him from the task given him by God. When he dies, it is to atone for the sins of men, not to overcome the evil forces of the world. When Mark reports that the Pharisees tempt Jesus by asking for a sign from heaven, Mark is drawing a picture of this evil generation which, in its human way, tries to corrupt the Son of God – a goal never reached.

A second item to be mentioned is the stress which Mark places on the deeds of Jesus as a witness to his messiahship. Mark's gospel is built around the activity of Jesus as Son of God and very little space is given to his teaching. The gospel of Jesus is not only the message which he proclaimed about the coming of the Kingdom of God, it is also the account of his passion and the events preceding it. As mentioned above, Mark is very careful to present Jesus as the Son of Man who exercises authority on earth, especially in the forgiving of sin and its related effects, the healing of disease and the exorcizing of demons.[17] The teaching of Jesus is designed to elaborate this aspect of Mark's presentation. Jesus is the Son of Man who, because of his suffering and death, has authority on earth; the future Son of Man, this same Jesus, is also the one who will judge. It is the death and resurrection which combine to clarify the significance of the deeds of Jesus, and Mark is merely making this as explicit as possible within the confines of the messianic secrecy motif. Thus, when we consider the Pharisees' request for a sign, it must be understood against the background of the many wonders which have already been performed. The persistent blindness of men is curable only when there is

---

[15] Ernest Best, *The Temptation and the Passion: the Markan Soteriology* (1965), esp. pp. 22f.

[16] James M. Robinson, *The Problem of History in Mark* (1957).

[17] Especially Mark 2.10 and 2.28.

openness toward the authority of Jesus (cf. Mark 8.22–26 and
10.46–52).

A third factor of importance is Mark's description of the way of
discipleship. The disciple is one who sees himself living in the
shadow of the cross. The pattern that emerges in chs. 8, 9 and 10
is quite clear: the announcement of the suffering Son of Man as
the meaning of messiahship demands an immediate explanation
about the risks involved in following this Messiah.[18] The disciple
is one who must be willing to go to the cross. In fact, to be a disciple is to accept *that* fate as a very real possibility (Mark. 8.34–36).
Since it is by the suffering of Christ that man has been reconciled
with God, the fate of the disciple may lie along the same path.
This is not a discipleship of preparation, or an ethic of martyrdom. Rather, Mark is aware of the delay of the parousia and of
the difficulties through which the fellowship must pass: he sees
their suffering as a participation in the life of the community
which is created by the suffering Son of God. The taking up of the
cross is an imitation of the suffering of Jesus: the willingness to
become a servant is defined in terms of the coming passion and
the whole central section of the gospel is summarized in the saying about service which is redemptive for many (10.45). Not only
does this clarify the problem of the requirements of discipleship,
it also points to the way in which Mark had integrated the teaching of Jesus with the deeds of Jesus – all presented in the form of a
narrative. Mark presents an ethic of participation and not one of
preparation.

## Matthew

The theology of Matthew's gospel is a more elusive thing than
is that of Mark and Luke. Matthew is a user of traditions in a way
that Mark and Luke are not. Mark is very careful in stating his
purpose; none but truly relevant facts are recorded. Or perhaps
we should say, all facts are made to fit the general plan he has
chosen. Luke on the other hand, though his purpose is just as
definite, uses his tradition in large blocks and seems more inclined to change the tradition to achieve his goal. Matthew, however, has conflated his material. He interweaves Mark with the Q
material and also with distinctive sayings and parables of his own,

---

[18] Cf. Perrin, *Redaction Criticism*.

the so-called M source.[19] Whether it is really necessary to decide if M is a written source or not, seems unlikely; M reflects Matthew's tradition and concerns and he seems to give it about the same weight of authority as Q.

There is one editorial feature of Matthew's gospel about which most scholars will agree: his creation of long discourses and their prominent position in the structure of his gospel.[20] There can be little doubt that Matthew is more interested in the teaching of Jesus, and its relation to his activity, than was Mark. The five discourses each end with specific formulae and certainly help to highlight the major sections of the gospel.[21] It is also agreed that the material placed between the speeches has been carefully composed to elaborate or develop the theme of the speeches. Thus Matthew's compositional activity is perhaps just as thorough, though not as single-minded, as the similar work of Mark and Luke.

It is clear that Matthew has made a definite shift in the eschatological teaching in relation to Mark. There is a decided tendency among scholars to speak of Matthew's work as produced by a community or, at least, completed within a community.[22] This is the first appearance of the word ἐκκλησία in the synoptic tradition,[23] and Matthew is careful to relate the sayings of Jesus to the situation of the church in the period between the resurrection and the parousia. He has certainly been influenced by the delay of the parousia, as the ending of the gospel illustrates.[24] The church must begin to develop its thinking in anticipation of a delayed *eschaton*, yet he does not seem to have shifted as far in this direction

[19] Cf. Kümmel, *Introduction,* on the gospel of Matthew.
[20] Kümmel, *Introduction,* pp. 75–80. B. W. Bacon, *Studies in Matthew* (1930), pp. 80–90.
[21] The five discourses are:
  1. Chs. 5–7 The Sermon on the Mount.
  2. Ch. 10 The Mission Discourse.
  3. Ch. 13 The Parables of the Kingdom.
  4. Ch. 18 The Discourse to the Disciples.
  5. Chs. 24–5 The Eschatological Discourse.
The concluding formula is καὶ ἐγένετο ὅτε ὁ Ἰησοῦς ἐτέλεσεν τοὺς λόγους τούτους.
[22] Krister Stendahl, *The School of St. Matthew and its Use of the Old Testament* (1954), pp. 30–5.
[23] Matt. 16.18.
[24] Cf. Conzelmann, *Outline,* p. 147, and G. Bornkamm, 'End-expectation and Church in Matthew', in G. Bornkamm, G. Barth and H. J. Held, *Tradition and Interpretation in Matthew* (1963), pp. 38–40.

as has Luke. The expectation of the end is still a major factor to be considered by the church, but the end awaited is not an imminent one; the life of the church in the present is a fact and must be seriously considered. Thus we might say that Matthew's eschatology stands between that of Mark and Luke.

One of the especially puzzling problems offered by Matthew is the specific environment in which he writes and the nature of his intended readers.[25] There have been many suggestions, from Jewish-Christian to Hellenistic-Christian. It is clear, if only from the end of the book, that the Gentile mission is an aspect of the work of the church, but there are hints throughout that the Jewish mission is part of his concern; or perhaps that he is part of a Jewish-Christian community. The church is defined as the true Israel and Matthew develops this idea toward a justification of the Gentile mission, i.e. the new Israel must take up the missionary task abandoned by the old Israel.[26] 'The theological principle at work here is that of promise and fulfilment.' There is no sharp break with Jewish traditions; continuity must be preserved. Jesus comes not to destroy but to fulfil the law. However, the fulfilment is not a continuation of the Jewish interpretation but a radical change in the understanding of that material *and* in its interpretation.[27] The distinctive character of the formulae used for quotations has been carefully analysed and although no common agreement has been reached, the careful way in which these quotations have been used indicates a tendency parallel to Luke's – the person of Jesus, the teacher and Lord, has demanded a reorientation and hence a reassessment of the Jewish background materials. Thus, old and new are intertwined in a complex way.[28]

Just as Matthew uses Mark's outline, he also adopts Mark's theology of the cross. His elaboration of this theme is careful and precise. Jesus is depicted as the one who moves toward the suffering of the cross; it is a characteristic of the disciple that he must expect to walk this same path. Matthew tends to follow Mark's statements that discipleship is the imitation of Jesus. It is the paradox of the lowliness of revelation which Matthew stresses, especially in the birth stories and the Beatitudes.[29] Conzelmann has pointed out that, according to Matthew, suffering and perse-

[25] Stendahl, *Matthew*, pp. 20–9; cf. also Conzelmann, *Outline*, p. 145.
[26] Conzelmann, *ibid.*      [27] *Ibid.*      [28] Stendahl, *Matthew*.
[29] Bornkamm, *Matthew*, pp. 36–8.

cution are really the way of life for those who wish to follow the commandment of love.[30] The life of Jesus is a preliminary, although definitive, statement of what the Christian can expect if he is to be a true follower. And in this sense as well, there is a continuity between the old Israel and the new.

Therefore, in the context of a well-defined anticipation of the reality of a future judgment which will vindicate the true Christian, Matthew must deal with the problem of the church in the present moment prior to the final consummation. Matthew is concerned about the impact of the coming judgment on the activity of the present moment and yet the church's relation to the history of Israel must also be considered.[31] The result is a recognition of Jesus as the suffering one who interprets the law; he is not the new lawgiver.[32] The Pharisees are hypocrites because they do not properly interpret the law; they have not paid attention to essential issues but have shifted attention toward the minutiae. Matthew emphasizes Jesus the teacher; his earthly function is to clarify the significance of the law and also to fulfil it by his obedience. Lowliness is the constant theme of Matthew's gospel.[33]

Matthew's recognition of the delay of the parousia is also evident in his expectation of the coming judgment of the church. The church is not the kingdom of God; it is the mixed community which will be purged at the judgment. But that judgment is based upon definite standards and it is for this purpose that the teaching of Jesus has practical implications for the present situation. The disciple lives in the present era between the resurrection and parousia; he follows the law as interpreted and lived by Jesus. When Matthew reports the call of the disciples they respond to the proclamation of the coming of the kingdom and not to the new interpretation of the law.[34] The *context* of discipleship is the expectation of judgment; the content of that life is the following of the law. Bornkamm notes that the summary in 28.20 states that the church is to make disciples and then teach them all that Jesus has taught.[35] The disciples, when they are sent out, proclaim the nearness of the kingdom of God (10.7).

Thus for Matthew, to speak of the church is to describe that community which anticipates the coming *eschaton,* although it is in

---

[30] Conzelmann, *Outline,* p. 146.        [31] Bornkamm, *Matthew,* p. 39.
[32] *Ibid.,* p. 35.        [33] *Ibid.,* p. 37.
[34] Matt. 10.1–7; Bornkamm, *Matthew,* pp. 40f.        [35] *Ibid.*

no sense a perfect community. Judgment falls upon the church, and those who are righteous are those who will survive. What then does it mean to be righteous? To be righteous and to be perfect seem to be equivalent terms for Matthew. Jesus is the prime example of both; it is for this reason that he is the Son of God and the Son of Man. Jesus accepts the law and points to its primary principles, and he lives them. He must suffer as a result of his obedience, but this is part of the perfection which God demands. Suffering and devotion to God is righteousness and perfection. Discipleship is not the way to perfection, but the very perfection that is demanded.[36]

## Luke

Any attempt to understand the theology of Luke must begin with the seminal work of Hans Conzelmann.[37] It is Conzelmann who has uncovered the basic theological character of Luke's gospel and all recent investigation of Luke stands either for or against his work.[38] Once we have a basic understanding of Conzelmann's picture of Luke, it will then be possible to ask about certain details which will be of interest to us in assessing the significance and meaning of the sign of Jonah.

Conzelmann describes Luke's thought as 'early catholic'.[39] In using this phrase he has a number of things in mind: the shift in eschatological thought, the shrinking of the term apostle to mean only the twelve. That is to say, he sees in Luke the beginning of a development which eventually results in what he calls Catholic Christianity. In this sense, Luke is certainly to be distinguished from the other evangelists, as his modifications of Mark make clear.

The most conspicuous evidence of Luke's reflection upon the tradition is his positive alteration of the eschatology of his sources.[40] The immediate expectation of the parousia is not maintained. Rather, the end has been delayed and the church must now reorient itself toward the present and take up the work demanded in the immediate future. Rather than accept the option chosen by

[36] Conzelmann, *Outline*, p. 147.
[37] Hans Conzelmann, *The Theology of St. Luke* (1961).
[38] Cf. the essays in Leander Keck and J. Louis Martyn, eds., *Studies in Luke-Acts. Essays presented in honor of Paul Schubert* (1966).
[39] Conzelmann, *Outline*, p. 149.      [40] Conzelmann, *Luke*, pp. 101–36.

John and Paul, Luke has a view of history called *Heilsgeschichte*. It has become a commonplace of New Testament study to view Luke as the greatest representative of the salvation-history solution to the problem of the delay of the parousia.[41] The end is not removed, it is merely part of the far distant future. The result of this change of perspective is to place positive emphasis on the present and to view the past as history, to be studied and analysed as history.

Conzelmann claims that this basic salvation-history orientation is expressed as a recognition of three epochs within the history of salvation.[42] The first is the period of Israel, the second is the period of Jesus which Conzelmann calls 'the mid-point of time', and the third is the period of the church, the time of the activity of the Holy Spirit. This threefold organization of material by Luke is evident in the distinct break which Luke makes between the time of Jesus and the time of the church. The resurrection and the ascension together form the conclusion of Jesus' ministry while the gift of the Spirit signals the beginning of the church. The church, as the time of the Spirit, anticipates the parousia but only in the sense of an event far off in the future. The church is definitely a part of God's plan of salvation, the time in which the gospel is spread from Judea to the ends of the earth. Luke does not know when the end will arrive, and it is not necessary to know. The church lives in its own age with its own plans which Luke sets forth in the second volume of his history. He deliberately looks ahead to the task of the church in the era just now beginning and, as a corollary, can look back to the life of Jesus as an event of the past. Luke's gospel is the first life of Jesus.[43]

In the gospel, Jesus announces the kingdom of God while the events of Jesus' life illustrate the fact that the kingdom of God has been announced; the wonders which Jesus performs, the fact of his resurrection and ascension, and the sending of the Spirit, all confirm that Jesus is the one who announced the kingdom of God. The life of Jesus is not presented as a guide or pattern to be imitated. The announcement of the kingdom of God has been completed and the Spirit now guides the church in the task of an eventual implementation of the mission programme, the announcement of the gospel.[44]

---

[41] Cullmann, *Salvation,* p. 46.　　[42] Conzelmann, *Outline,* p. 151.
[43] *Ibid.*　　　　　[44] *Ibid.*

Alongside the conscious modification of the eschatology of Mark, Luke has a much more historical understanding of the development of the life of Jesus. The clues to this redaction by Luke lie in the geographical references in the gospel.[45] Conzelmann argues that Luke uses geographical notations with theological overtones. The insertion of the travel narrative (9.51–18.14) is Luke's method of indicating a development in the thought of Jesus, from the Galilean period when Jesus is conscious of being the Messiah, to the Judean period when he understands himself to be the one who is to suffer. The movement from Galilee to Jerusalem is the movement toward the place where the suffering, death and resurrection are to occur. Jesus is thereby accepting the fate of the suffering Son of Man. The period in Jerusalem is the time of Jesus' self-recognition as king; it opens with the triumphal entry and is completed in the resurrection appearances, all of which take place in Jerusalem and not in Galilee. Satan is bound at the beginning of the ministry (4.13), and he reappears in the passion story (22.3) to force the necessary death and resurrection of the Messiah as king.[46]

The gift of the Spirit establishes the church as the true Israel, a church which has its origin and centre of operation in Jerusalem, where Jesus appeared and where, after his departure, the Spirit is given. Although Jesus restricts his ministry to Israel, the new age demands that the message be spread to the ends of the earth, always under the impulse of the Spirit.[47]

Within this general framework there are a number of specific issues which we must raise in anticipation of the sign of Jonah.

First is Luke's attitude toward his sources. A glance at an outline of a synopsis of the gospels shows that Luke has a tendency to use his sources in large blocks.[48] Even though he uses the Markan outline of the ministry of Jesus, he incorporates other material by inserting it, for the most part, as large units and does not scatter it throughout the Markan sequence.[49] In this process, Luke is careful to show the relationship between events; he anticipates future sayings and events by redactional additions. We would expect that Luke has felt free to modify or change the wording of Mark to make it read more smoothly or to remove or translate

---

[45] *Ibid.*, pp. 151f.; also *Luke*, pp. 27–94.
[46] *Luke*, p. 199.     [47] *Ibid.*, also *Outline*, pp. 151f.
[48] Cf. Kümmel, *Introduction*, p. 92.     [49] *Ibid.*, p. 97.

inappropriate words and phrases. Luke does not make many emendations in the words ascribed to Jesus; those words are usually copied from Mark without much variation. It is usually supposed that he is reworking the material for Greek-speaking readers. None the less, Luke indicates his theological inclinations, first by using *kyrios* as a title for Jesus and secondly by stressing the messiahship of Jesus. He also stresses Jesus' sympathy and concern for both men and women.[50] All of this would indicate that Luke maintains the order of the Q material more readily than Matthew and that he is closer to the original wording of Q only in the words ascribed to Jesus. He changes or adapts the setting but not the saying.

Secondly, and of more importance for our concern, is Luke's failure to adopt the Markan soteriological *paradidomi* tradition.[51] Luke has been careful to modify the very significant statement in Mark 10.45: 'For the Son of Man also came not to be served but to serve, and to give his life as a ransom for many.' Luke's corresponding passage (22.27) reads: 'For which is the greater, one who sits at table, or one who serves? Is it not the one who sits at table? But I am among you as one who serves.' Conzelmann comments on this unusual aspect of Luke's theology: '. . . there is no trace of any passion mysticism, nor is any direct soteriological significance drawn from Jesus' suffering or death. There is no suggestion of a connection with the forgiveness of sins.'[52] Luke emphasizes an element from his tradition, i.e. the necessity of the passion, and makes it significant within the fullness of God's plan. The word δεῖ is crucial for Luke; the life of Jesus, though it is the 'mid-point of time', is still a part of the full and extensive plan which God has for his people.[53] For the community, of course, the work of Jesus is identical with that of the Father, and both God and Jesus are described as Lord.[54] The death of Jesus is not the essence of the saving event; it is merely the pathway to glory. Undoubtedly this is 'a paradoxical manifestation of glory'.[55] But the passion and suffering which are part of Luke's tradition are interpreted from the view of the whole plan of God throughout the life of Jesus. Luke is not devising a new approach; he is developing an *under-*

---

[50] *Ibid.*, pp. 97–102.
[51] Tödt, *Son of Man*, pp. 151f., 155–94; Conzelmann, *Luke*, pp. 201–6.
[52] Conzelmann, *Luke*, p. 201.
[53] *Ibid.*, p. 153.    [54] *Ibid.*, p. 184.    [55] *Ibid.*, p. 196.

*standing* of the passion which is part of the material he receives.
And he does not emphasize, indeed he even deletes, material
which would lead to a more Pauline interpretation. For instance,
the anointing at Bethany is missing in Luke, but Satan reappears
(22.3). The Last Supper also becomes a time in which the disciples
are prepared for the period of conflict which is now beginning.
Participation in the supper is a central concern for the community
now that Jesus is seated at the right hand of God and now that they
are in possession of the Spirit.[56] Thus, by not following the Markan
passion soteriology, Luke has indicated that his heritage lies with
the style of theology represented by Q. This factor will become
especially important when we come to the Lukan version of the
sign of Jonah.

Thirdly, we must take account of Luke's understanding of
discipleship. Since it is only through the church that one can be a
disciple, the church becomes an integral part of God's plan of
salvation. The church functions as the mediator between God and
man and can also overcome the problem of extended time before
the end – in the fellowship, in sacraments and in prayer. Part of the
immediate situation of the church is the threat of martyrdom, and
this leads him to develop an ethic of martyrdom.[57] The early
church is portrayed as an aspect of the action of God, and Luke
creates the possibility, which is later realized, of including the
church within the confession of the full plan of God, i.e. the third
article of the creed. But the disciple is not expected to become a
Spirit-filled ecstatic. Rather, since the parousia has been delayed,
the emphasis is placed on the 'way' into the kingdom.[58] The
disciple hears the proclamation and follows in the way, with God's
help. The message informs the hearer of the coming judgment and
of the fact that he is a sinner. Thus when Luke reports the preaching, its content is usually a call for repentance and conversion,
motivated by the judgment.[59] Forgiveness is likewise a predominant idea in Luke, based upon the condition of repentance. A
combination of repentance and conversion, which together form the
basis for baptism and forgiveness[60] indicates a change of attitude
and way of life. 'Attitude and behaviour are distinguished';[61] the
*way* of the disciple is a separate item alongside correct doctrine.
Conzelmann stresses that this is a report of what would actually

56 *Ibid.*, p. 200.     57 *Ibid.*, p. 210.     58 *Ibid.*, p. 227.
59 *Ibid.*     60 *Ibid.*, p. 229.     61 *Ibid.*

be happening in the early church as the result of its preaching.[62] But this is merely the beginning of discipleship, not the full life of the Christian; the church and the Spirit act as a bridge to the future, to the *eschaton*. The Spirit is the guarantee that forgiveness has been received, but it is not the blessing of salvation. The problem of the delay is therefore solved: the Spirit is a promise which can make less significant the passage of time.[63]

The period after conversion is that time in the life of the disciple when the 'ethical element begins to stand out in its own right.'[64] Judgment remains as a factor because it is a future reality, not because it is imminent. It is for this reason that Luke does not recommend an *imitatio Christi* but rather asks that things be done 'for my sake'.[65] The times have changed and Luke moves in the direction of an ethic of martyrdom.

If we were to sum up the basic characteristics of discipleship for Luke it would have to be described as 'new era life'. Suffering is an integral part of the new era though it is not redemptive. It is a consequence of living according to the 'new era' programme under the realization of the judgment, which, though distant, *will* take place.

It is necessary to emphasize the significance of the warning about the judgment which is a threat from the distant future. It is a simple matter for Luke to accept the tradition of Q without much apparent modification because he is concerned with the description of the preaching done in the early church. Even though the judgment is not imminent for Luke, it is none the less real and is a major factor in initiating repentance and confession among the contemporaries of Luke. Jesus does not only preach the coming of the kingdom but the content of the life of the kingdom as well. Those who respond to that message must be fully aware of the threat of the *eschaton* and must reorient themselves appropriately. Thus Jesus is best described as one who teaches and warns about the end and then later, after his vindication as Lord, supplies the means whereby that new orientation to life can be made a reality, through the Spirit. The Christian is prepared for the end by being acquainted with Jesus' proclamation. As Conzelmann says, the shift is toward an ethical concern.[66]

A fourth element of interest is the use Luke makes of the Old Testament. The separation between the present epoch and the

[62] *Ibid.*     [63] *Ibid.*, p. 230.     [64] *Ibid.*, p. 231.     [65] *Ibid.*, p. 233.     [66] *Ibid.*, p. 232.

past is maintained, but the redemptive plan of God integrates the past and the present. Elements of the former era pass over into the present era. Conzelmann states that Luke does not consider the prophecy of the Old Testament extending to the *eschaton* but only to the giving of the Spirit.[67] It is the event of the resurrection which now clarifies the Old Testament prophecies, as Luke 24 illustrates.[68] The Jew cannot be expected to see fully before that point; but from now on, he is responsible for his blindness. It is easy for Luke, with his more historical perspective, to assume that the era of guilt really only begins with the start of the third period of God's plan. In the new era, the church can look back upon the significance of God's promise and now can understand that Jesus fulfils God's plan. Thus, Jonah can illustrate the correspondence between the Old Testament and the New, Jonah in the period of Israel, and Jesus in the 'mid-point of time'. Luke has no difficulty in adopting Q and its use of the Old Testament as a way of opening insight into the real significance of Jesus. But the Jonah story is primarily warning about the capability of God to complete his plan. Jonah and Jesus are both great preachers who were vindicated. It is a warning to take Jesus and his vindication seriously: the end will be real, although it is still far off in the future. The Ninevites repented; Israel should follow in the same path. Luke sees the continuity as the appeal for repentance under the threat of judgment; Jonah is a sign 'to the Ninevites' because he preached (cf. 11.32).

A fifth and final element of Luke's theology must be stressed – his use of the future Son of Man sayings. We have already noted that Luke does not emphasize an apocalyptic eschatology and that, when he uses it, it is a report of a saying of the past. Tödt argues that Luke is transferring the older terminology into a Christian Hellenistic situation.[69] As we would expect, the future Son of Man is relegated to the distant future, and the distinction between Jesus and the Son of Man is maintained. The apocalyptic Son of Man is now continuous with the suffering Son of Man, at successive stages, and the future Son of Man is really part of the transcendent world. The future verb, used to describe the future Son of Man, is a historic report of the past and is not a reflection of an imminent expectation. The essence of Luke's theology rests upon the significance of Jesus in his earthly ministry, completed in the

[67] *Ibid.*, p. 161.     [68] *Ibid.*, p. 162.     [69] Tödt, *Son of Man*, pp. 108–9.

past. The details of that ministry – his teaching, deeds and saving activity – are the really decisive factors. Luke is more inclined to transmit Jesus' teaching as he received it and to incorporate it into the scheme which he sees as the plan of God.

## THE THEOLOGY OF THE Q COMMUNITY

### *Tödt's Contribution to an Understanding of Q*

Tödt was led to a consideration of Q by the results of his redaction-critical approach to the Son of Man sayings.[70] The absence of suffering sayings in the Q material highlighted an issue which had already been recognized on the basis of other evidence, viz. the distinctiveness of the non-passion christology of Q. Tödt finds in Q a very definite, but at the same time distinctive, christological concern. In Mark, two strands of christology, passion and non-passion, are co-ordinated in the suffering Son of Man sayings. If Q does not have an interest in suffering sayings, and if Mark was the first to create this co-ordination, then an understanding of the theological stance of Q may explain the origin of the Son of Man christology. The task, then, is to determine the significance of the Son of Man sayings in Q and the role they play in the full theological programme of the Q community. To set the analysis in context, Tödt surveys the history of the critical evaluation of Q.[71]

Research on Q really begins with Harnack's *The Sayings of Jesus*. Harnack's work illustrates that the Markan hypothesis had made immediately evident the distinctive quality of the Q material in contrast to the passion kerygma of Mark. The teachings of Jesus come primarily from Q and hence Q's great significance for Harnack. His analysis has been illustrated above,[72] and we need only mention here that, as we might expect, Harnack *de*-emphasizes the eschatological tendencies in Q. The problem, as Harnack see it, is the sayings of Jesus versus the passion kerygma.

Bultmann and Dibelius both focus attention on the kerygma and seek to establish its theological priority.[73] As a result they are less interested in the non-passion Q material. Both see the problem only in relation to the more central problem of the establishment of

---

[70] Cf. ch. I, p. 20, above.     [71] Cf. ch. I, pp. 21f., above.
[72] Cf. ch. I, pp. 8ff., above.     [73] Tödt, *Son of Man*, pp. 238–41.

the kerygma. Dibelius goes to the extreme of claiming that the Q material has no claim to significance on its own because it does not have any indication of the passion history. Q is theologically and chronologically secondary; after the realization that the parousia is delayed the church turns to the problem of moral instruction. Q supplements the real core of the tradition and must have been compiled at a later stage in the development of the early church. Perhaps the most telling indication of the lack of Q's theological significance for Dibelius is his use of the word *halakha* to characterize the type of material Q represents: '. . . the sayings of Jesus were originally gathered together for a hortatory end, to give the Churches advice, help and commandment by means of the Master's words.'[74]

Later, Tödt points out, Dibelius associates the tradition of the Lord's sayings with the community's belief in the validity of Jesus' eschatological teaching. This means that the sayings are transmitted as Jesus' instruction for the church in the light of the imminent coming of God's kingdom – *not* simply as rules for life. Thus Tödt implies that the eschatological perspective which Harnack rejected becomes a key factor in the developing reassessment of Q.[75]

Bultmann categorizes Q as 'Jesus' eschatological proclamation'.[76] None the less, he stresses the priority of the passion kerygma in the church and the Jewishness of Jesus' teaching. The continuity of Jesus' words and the community's kerygma is denied. Jesus was not understood messianically at the earliest stage; his messiahship was purely future.[77] The evidence for this assessment is Q. But, Tödt asks, why was Q collected in the first place? Why were the sayings of Jesus collected? Isn't the voice of the risen one good enough for the church?

Tödt next turns to T. W. Manson's *The Sayings of Jesus*.[78] Manson follows suit in stressing the passion kerygma and asserts that it was the central theme from the start. The church only later turns to Jesus' words when she needs a way of fixing a norm for her way of life. Here Manson is quite close to Dibelius' original position. Of the four possible motives for collecting the sayings, Manson claims that the first is by far the most influential:

[74] Dibelius, *Tradition,* p. 246.    [75] Tödt, *Son of Man,* p. 237.
[76] Quoted by Tödt, *ibid.,* p. 240.    [77] *Ibid.,* pp. 240f.
[78] *Ibid.,* pp. 241–5.

1. Pastoral care.
2. Personal interest in Jesus.
3. Apologetic use in the Gentile world.
4. Defence against subversive doctrines in Palestine.

Manson also acknowledges two basic streams of tradition – the passion-resurrection kerygma and the 'authoritative teacher' material.[79]

Manson goes further, though, picking up hints from Harnack, when he claims that he can find a pattern in the arrangement of Q. Since we have most of Q, and since Luke appears to be closer to the original text, Luke's arrangement is provisionally accepted and later declared to be authentic. Manson notices that the arrangement in Q parallels that of 'M' in four places. Matthew has apparently used Q to fill in and supplement his source, M; while Luke, on the other hand, has retained, to a fair degree, the original order of Q. Thus, an outline of a pre-Q and pre-M level of tradition is uncovered:

1. Jesus' preaching.
2. Mission charge.
3. Against the Pharisees.
4. Eschatological speech.

The obvious distinctiveness is, of course, the lack of a passion account. Why? Manson's explanation is that those who used this collection already knew it! But, asks Tödt, why is there no mention or hint of this prerequisite in Q?[80]

Manson also makes quite a point of the small amount of polemical or controversy material in Q (10 per cent). He explains this by saying that the positive approach is better than the disputing approach.[81] But as Tödt is quick to note, although there are no developed controversy dialogues, there very definitely is a tension in Q; Jesus stands over against both the Jewish authorities and 'this generation'. Tödt concludes by asking how we are to conceive of the relationship between the kerygma and Q.[82] Manson has not solved the problem for him.

Why will not the exhortation solution work? Because of the

[79] Tödt, *Son of Man*, p. 242.
[80] *Ibid.*, pp. 243f., quoting Manson, *Sayings*, p. 16.
[81] Manson, *Sayings*, p. 16.
[82] Tödt, *Son of Man*, pp. 243–5.

presence in Q of such material as the Beelzebul controversy, the
Jonah sayings, and the prophecy about Jerusalem. What role can
this material have played in an exhortation collection?[83]

A big step forward, as Tödt sees it, is made by Bultmann when
he observes that Jesus' teaching was not only gathered, it was proclaimed.[84] If it is taught, rather than used as a moral guide, we
must conceive of a community not centred on the kerygma, one
which understands its task as that of continuing to proclaim the
message which Jesus proclaimed. The words of Jesus (and not
just his death) would now have significance.

How can we get at the motives that resulted in the Q collection?
Tödt suggests that we look first at the mission discourse in
Matthew and Luke, which is based on Q, and compare it to Mark.

Matthew and Luke show the Q influence primarily in Matt. 10.7
(= Luke 10.9) where the disciples are told to pass on the message
which Jesus has been preaching – the near approach of the kingdom of God. Mark 1.1 states that the message is about Jesus the
Christ. When the disciples are commissioned to preach, the influence of Q in Matthew and Luke is obvious. This means that
they consider the announcement of the coming of the kingdom of
God to be as relevant now (in the community after Easter) as it
was in Jesus' lifetime. Mark, with his concern for the passion, finds
little place for the proclamation of the coming kingdom. The
nature of Q is determined by the imminence of God's reign and
not by the passion kerygma. It is for this reason, then, that the Q
community looks for the coming Son of Man. Because Tödt con-
siders the future sayings authentic,[85] the relation between Jesus
and Q is no problem. Whether we accept the coming sayings as
authentic or not does not detract from the force of their existence
in Q. Tödt's point is that the expectation of the Q community is
highlighted by its use of the Son of Man title and the related statement of the nature of the mission of the disciples.

The problem of the relation of the passion kerygma to the continuance of the teaching of Jesus is solved by Tödt when he argues
that the kerygma enables those in the Q community to continue
to proclaim the message Jesus proclaimed.[86] The resurrection is

[83] *Ibid.,* p. 246.
[84] *Ibid.,* p. 247, and Rudolf Bultmann, *Theology of The New Testament* I
(1951), p. 34.
[85] Tödt., *Son of Man,* pp. 57, 112, and elsewhere.
[86] *Ibid.,* p. 251.

understood as Jesus' turning anew in love toward his own, even after they had denied the fellowship which had existed while Jesus was alive. Rather than preach the resurrection, the resurrection leads them to preach the fellowship which Jesus promised. The gift of salvation is the renewed fellowship which is continuous with the fellowship which existed previously. The resurrection is assumed by the Q community to be the validation of the gift of fellowship. Tödt suggests that the comparative lateness of the resurrection narratives is to be explained by the simple fact that the earliest preaching was not passion kerygma but Jesus' words; there was no need to develop a resurrection narrative.[87]

Thus, although the resurrection is of crucial significance for the Q community, it is not a subject of the early preaching. The resurrection affirms Jesus' authority and thereby also the fellowship bestowed by Jesus, his teaching, and Jesus himself. In Tödt's words, 'Christological cognition had occurred'.[88] Jesus, as the coming Son of Man, is he who will renew the fellowship. The continuity between Jesus and the risen Lord lies in the equating of Jesus and the Son of Man. It is an easy step from this recognition of Jesus as continuous with the Son of Man to the creation of the present-activity Son of Man sayings; Jesus' authority is now recognized as having been present in his earthly ministry. It should be noted that Tödt places marked significance on Mark 8.38 and par. for this discussion of the centrality of discipleship and fellowship in Q.[89] These 'sentences of holy law' have been placed by Käsemann in the early Christian eucharist.[90] If this is correct, it would raise the significance of the table fellowship in the early church and perhaps explain the more specific origins of the whole Q theological enterprise. Norman Perrin has argued that the table fellowship played a crucial role in the life of Jesus and in the early church.[91] Perhaps we can also see here how it might have led to the whole Q theological emphasis.

With this background, Tödt proceeds to examine some specific Q sayings.[92] He wants to show that there is an attachment to Jesus in the Son of Man sayings and elsewhere in Q. If the earliest

[87] *Ibid.*        [88] *Ibid.*, p. 252.        [89] *Ibid.*, pp. 250–3.

[90] Ernst Käsemann, 'Sentences of Holy Law in the New Testament', *New Testament Questions of Today* (1969), pp. 66–81. See below for a full discussion.

[91] Perrin, *Rediscovering*, pp. 102–8.

[92] Tödt, *Son of Man*, pp. 253–65.

christological cognition is the relating of the future Son of Man to Jesus, it is to the Jesus who taught, not to the Jesus who died. The fellowship forms around the Jesus who is about to come as Son of Man and not around the Jesus who died; it is an eschatological fellowship and not a passion fellowship. This as he notes, stands in opposition to Bultmann's separation of the teacher from his teaching. Jesus is significant not merely because he *will be* the Son of Man but because the one who will be the Son of Man is the teacher whose words now become important in the fellowship which expects the imminent appearance of the Son of Man, that is, Jesus.

The analysis of this material, claims Tödt, clarifies the importance of attachment to Jesus; access to Jesus is access to the coming salvation. Jesus guarantees this fellowship. The title Son of Man serves in Q as an equivalent to Jesus. Jesus speaks not only as the risen one but also as the earthly teacher who acts effectively by means of his word.[93]

Why is there tension between Jesus and this world? Because of Jesus' authority. Jesus is portrayed not as the one who gives his blood for the community but as the teacher who summons men by means of the challenge to follow him. To be guilty is to repudiate the message and to ignore the claim that is made. It is the presence of Jesus that creates the tension; but 'the future is determined by the effect of his presence'.[94]

What use is made of the Old Testament in Q? There is no reference to the passion kerygma. There is a 'typical' emphasis on the judgment against this generation because of the presence of Jesus and because of the future salvation or its loss.[95] Jesus' authority is not recognized by his contemporaries. Q and the Son of Man as judge belong together.

Is it possible to recover the order of Q? Tödt claims that Q was arranged thematically and that Matthew and Luke both see some meaning in this because they both seem to conform to it.[96]

Matthew, in composing speeches, is led by Q (partially) since it offered the foundation for the Sermon on the Mount, the mission discourse, etc. Matthew combines the parousia sayings with Mark 13; Luke places this material after the travel narrative and prior to the Judean period. Luke adds parousia material after using Mark

---

[93] *Ibid.,* pp. 264f.  [94] *Ibid.,* p. 266.
[95] *Ibid.,* pp. 266–9.  [96] *Ibid.,* pp. 269f.

13, that is, he ends the apocalyptic discourse with Son of Man references.

Q preserves the eschatological teaching more than any other stratum of tradition. Once Jesus is recognized as the coming Son of Man, these future sayings are arranged in a group with the exception of two units: Luke 12.8f. = Matt. 10.32f. (Confession-Denial) and Luke 11.30–32 = Matt. 12.40–42 (the Sign of Jonah). Matt. 19.28 (Twelve Thrones) and Matt. 10.23 (Flee that City) would also belong in this category provided that they were found in some form or other in Q.[97]

Luke 12.8f. = Matt. 10.32f. is placed by Matthew in the context of fearless speaking and near the mission discourse (mostly from Q). Thus, since the pointing to the parousia is not the primary intent, the saying really does belong here. Matthew may have preserved Q's order better than Luke at this point.[98]

The Jonah saying is the other future Son of Man saying which is outside the parousia collection (Luke 11.30–32 and par.). But there is evidence that this demand for a sign was already connected to the Beelzebul pericope in Q. Parousia is a secondary concern for this saying also.[99]

Tödt concludes that the Q ordering was not indiscriminate but planned, that the coming Son of Man is integral to Q and that Q's order is respected by Matthew and Luke.

The significance of Tödt's work is far-reaching and will be important in any future discussion of the theology of Q. The following sections of this chapter present my further suggestions about the theology of the Q community. It is this further insight into the theological *Sitz im Leben* of Q which will assist in solving the puzzle of the Sign of Jonah.

## The Eschatological Correlative

Discussion concerning the origin and use of the title 'Son of Man' has been long and involved – and shows no signs of waning. The generally accepted approach is the one assumed by Tödt and first proposed by Rudolf Bultmann: the synoptic sayings can be divided into three categories: (1) those which state the present activity or authority of the Son of Man, (2) those which refer to his future activity, and (3) those which refer to his suffering and

---

[97] *Ibid.*, pp. 270f.    [98] *Ibid.*    [99] *Ibid.*, p. 271.

resurrection.[100] This analysis of the sayings is also the point from which this study will proceed.[101]

One of the major contributions of Tödt's work on Q has been his clarifying of the significance of the Son of Man sayings in the Q tradition. He has argued that the Son of Man title was first used in Q as a reference to the future Son of Man who will come as judge.[102] He accepts Bultmann's decision about the authenticity of the future Son of Man sayings and argues that they are indeed authentic because of the distinction made in each saying between Jesus and the Son of Man. This differentiation is not typical of the early church and represents a hold-over from an earlier level of tradition.[103] But when the authority of Jesus is recognized, when it becomes clear to this community that Jesus and the now risen Son of Man are one and the same, the Q community creates sayings such as those in Luke 7.34, Luke 12.10 and Luke 9.58, which stress the present activity of the Son of Man. It makes specific statements about the continuity of the historical Jesus and the Son of Man who is to come, who is now exalted at the right hand of God. The gift of salvation is the renewed fellowship of the community, a fellowship that centres on the table fellowship which Jesus instituted while on earth. 'The resurrection is God's affirmation of Jesus' *exousia*. Thereby the resurrection also is the confirmation before God of the fellowship bestowed by Jesus in his *exousia* on his own. Thus it is comprehensible why Jesus' teaching was taken up again and continued to be taught by the community; what Jesus had said had been confirmed by God'.[104] 'Christological cognition' occurs when the renewed teaching of Jesus' message is differentiated from his authentic teaching. Now the community can begin to make explicit the connection between the earthly Jesus and the risen Son of Man. In this way, present-activity sayings can be formulated; Jesus has *exousia* while on earth.

One of the major points at issue is the authenticity of the future Son of Man sayings. Tödt has been challenged on his assumption

---

[100] *Ibid.* Also Rudolf Bultmann, *The Theology of the New Testament* I, p. 30. Cf. Perrin, *Rediscovering,* for further discussion and bibliography.

[101] Other major positions are represented by E. Schweizer, 'The Son of Man', *JBL* LXXIX (1960), 119–29; Philipp Vielhauer, 'Jesus und der Menschensohn: Zur Diskussion mit Heinz Eduard Tödt und Eduard Schweizer', *ZThK* LX (1963), 133–77; F. H. Borsch, *The Son of Man in Myth and History* (1967); Morna D. Hooker, *The Son of Man in Mark* (1967).

[102] Tödt, p. 270.     [103] *Ibid.,* p. 273.     [104] *Ibid.,* p. 252.

of their authenticity by Vielhauer and Perrin.[105] The problem is a crucial one. If there is some indication that the community is the source of the future Son of Man sayings, it will obviously constitute a major clue to the theological tendency of that community. There can be no doubt about the significance of the future sayings and their juxtaposition within Q with the present-activity sayings.

One factor which has been previously overlooked is the common form which four of the six future Son of Man sayings contain. I propose to call this form an 'eschatological correlative'.

A correlative construction is one which brings together two items or persons in order to show a reciprocal relationship between them. The standard correlative form would be: As is the case with A, so it is with B. The correlative comparison is a common feature of Koine Greek.[106] However, the tense of the verb in the two clauses often does not show any great variation; a past tense in the protasis is often followed by the same tense in the apodosis, although at times, the apodosis contains a present tense. It is relatively uncommon to find a correlative in which the apodosis contains the future tense while a present or past tense stands in the protasis. It is precisely this 'past/future' or 'present/future' pattern which we find in these Q sayings and which I have called an eschatological correlative.

In summary form the eschatological correlative is:

Protasis: καθὼς (ὥσπερ, ὡς) – verb in past or present tense
Apodosis: οὕτως (κατὰ τὰ αὖτα) – ἔσται – ὁ υἱὸς τοῦ ἀνθρώπου.

This form occurs four times in Q:

| 1. Luke 11.30 | = Matt. 12.40: |
|---|---|
| καθὼς γὰρ ἐγένετο ὁ ᾽Ιωνᾶς τοῖς Νινευείταις σημεῖον, | ὥσπερ γὰρ ἦν ᾽Ιωνᾶς ἐν τῇ κοιλίᾳ τοῦ κήτους τρεῖς ἡμέρας καὶ τρεῖς νύκτας, |
| οὕτως ἔσται καὶ ὁ υἱὸς τοῦ ἀνθρώπου τῇ γενεᾷ ταύτῃ. | οὕτως ἔσται ὁ υἱὸς τοῦ ἀνθρώπου ἐν τῇ καρδίᾳ τῆς γῆς τρεῖς ἡμέρας καὶ τρεῖς νύκτας. |

105 Perrin, 'Son of Man', pp. i–iv, and *Rediscovering,* pp. 164–98; Philipp Vielhauer, 'Gottesreich und Menschensohn in der Verkündigung Jesu', in W. Schneemelcher, ed., *Festschrift für Gunther Dehn* (1957), pp. 51–79, and 'Jesus und der Menschensohn' (cited above).

106 F. W. Blass and A. Debrunner, *A Greek Grammar of the New Testament and other Early Christian Literature,* trans. from 9th–10th German ed. (1961),

2. Luke 17.24                          = Matt. 24.27:

ὥσπερ γὰρ ἡ ἀστραπὴ ἀστράπ-          ὥσπερ γὰρ ἡ ἀστραπὴ ἐξέρχεται
τουσα ἐκ τῆς ὑπὸ τὸν οὐρανὸν         ἀπὸ ἀνατολῶν καὶ φαίνεται ἕως
εἰς τὴν ὑπ᾽ οὐρανὸν λάμπει,          δυσμῶν,

**οὕτως ἔσται ὁ υἱὸς τοῦ ἀνθρώπου**   **οὕτως ἔσται** ἡ παρουσία **τοῦ υἱοῦ**
ἐν τῇ ἡμέρᾳ αὐτοῦ.                   **τοῦ ἀνθρώπου.**


3. Luke 17.26                          = Matt. 24.37:

καὶ **καθὼς** ἐγένετο ἐν ταῖς ἡμέραις  ὥσπερ δὲ αἱ ἡμέραι τοῦ **Νῶε,**
**Νῶε,**

**οὕτως ἔσται** καὶ ἐν ταῖς ἡμέραις    **οὕτως ἔσται** ἡ παρουσία **τοῦ**
**τοῦ υἱοῦ τοῦ ἀνθρώπου**              **υἱοῦ τοῦ ἀνθρώπου.**


4. Luke 17.28 and 30                   = Matt. 24.38f.:

ὁμοίως **καθὼς** ἐγένετο ἐν ταῖς       ὡς γὰρ ἦσαν ἐν ταῖς ἡμέραις
ἡμέραις Λώτ . . .                    [ἐκείναις] ταῖς πρὸ τοῦ
                                     κατακλυσμοῦ . . .

**κατὰ τὰ αὐτὰ ἔσται** ᾗ ἡμέρᾳ **ὁ υἱὸς**   **οὕτως ἔσται** καὶ ἡ παρουσία **τοῦ**
**τοῦ ἀνθρώπου** ἀποκαλύπτεται.        **υἱοῦ τοῦ ἀνθρώπου.**


The eschatological correlative occurs only once in the synoptics
outside Q:

Matt. 13.40f.:

**ὥσπερ** οὖν συλλέγεται τὰ ζιζάνια καὶ πυρὶ κατακαίεται,

**οὕτως ἔσται** ἐν τῇ συντελείᾳ τοῦ αἰῶνος.

ἀποστελεῖ **ὁ υἱὸς τοῦ ἀνθρώπου** τοὺς ἀγγέλους αὐτοῦ, . . .


These four eschatological correlative sayings in Q comprise
four of the six future Son of Man sayings in Q:

1. Luke 11.30    = Matt. 12.40    The Sign of Jonah.
2. Luke 17.24    = Matt. 24.27    The lightning.
3. Luke 17.26    = Matt. 24.37    Noah.
4. Luke 17.28, 30 = Matt. 24.38f.  Lot and Noah.

---

p. 236 (§453.1.) J. H. Moulton, *A Grammar of New Testament Greek,* Vol. III:
*Syntax,* by Nigel Turner (1963), p. 320.

5. Luke 12.39f.

... εἰ ᾔδει ὁ οἰκοδεσπότης ποίᾳ
ὥρᾳ ὁ κλέπτης ἔρχεται, ...

καὶ ὑμεῖς γίνεσθε ἔτοιμοι, ὅτι ᾗ
ὥρᾳ οὐ δοκεῖτε ὁ υἱὸς τοῦ
ἀνθρώπου ἔρχεται.

= Matt. 24.43f.:

... εἰ ᾔδει ὁ οἰκοδεσπότης ποίᾳ
φυλακῇ ὁ κλέπτης ἔρχεται ...

διὰ τοῦτο καὶ ὑμεῖς γίνεσθε
ἔτοιμοι, ὅτι ᾗ οὐ δοκεῖτε ὥρᾳ
ὁ υἱὸς τοῦ ἀνθρώπου ἔρχεται.

6. Luke 12.8

λέγω δὲ ὑμῖν, πᾶς ὃς ἂν ὁμολογήσῃ
ἐν ἐμοὶ ἔμπροσθεν τῶν
ἀνθρώπων,

καὶ ὁ υἱὸς τοῦ ἀνθρώπου
ὁμολογήσει ἐν αὐτῷ ἔμπροσθεν
τῶν ἀγγέλων τοῦ Θεοῦ ...

= Matt. 10.32:

πᾶς οὖν ὅστις ὁμολογήσει ἐν ἐμοὶ
ἔμπροσθεν τῶν ἀνθρωπων,

ὁμολογήσω κἀγὼ ἐν αὐτῷ
ἔμπροσθεν τοῦ πατρός μου τοῦ
ἐν τοῖς οὐρανοῖς ...

One of the more striking features of this form is its limited use in the synoptics. The eschatological correlative occurs these four times in Q, once in Matt. 13.40f. and never in Mark. In Matt. 13.40f. the form is broken; the Son of Man is mentioned in 13.41 and not in the apodosis of the correlative. It seems clear that Matthew has taken over the form and used it here in the interpretation of a parable; yet, he retains the formal structure for the most part *and* the Son of Man context in which it occurs in Q. The editorial activities of Matthew and Luke are also evident in the four Q sayings. Matthew prefers 'the parousia of the Son of Man' while Luke consistently says 'the day(s) of the Son of Man'. In the Jonah comparison the content has obviously been greatly modified, but the formal characteristics of the eschatological correlative remain intact.

Outside the synoptics, the occurrence of this form is just as interesting. In the fourth gospel, the καθώς (ὥσπερ) . . . οὕτως . . . correlative construction occurs six times; never, however, does the *eschatological* correlative occur, i.e. with the verb of the apodosis in the future tense. John refers to the Son of Man once with the correlative in 3.14, comparing the lifting up of the Son of Man to the lifting up of the serpent by Moses. In four other places (5.12; 5.26; 12.50; 14.31) where the correlative is used, Jesus is not referred to as the Son of Man, but rather is either explicitly called Son or speaks in the first person as the Son ('Father' having been mentioned in the protasis). Finally in the sixth occurrence of the correlative (15.4) the branch of the vine is correlated with the disciples.

The Johannine evidence would indicate that we have reached a later stage in the development of 'Son' christology. The form is used in part, but the apocalyptic elements have been removed. Once the form is established it can be filled with varying theological content.

Paul makes extensive use of the correlative but only in three places does the apodosis contain the future verb: Rom. 5.19, I Cor. 15.22 and 15.49. In every case he is comparing Christ and Adam. In Rom. 5.19 Paul compares the significance of Christ's obedience with Adam's disobedience; the gift of life has been given to us through Christ, just as death reigned through Adam's trespass. In I Cor. 15.22 and 15.49 Paul uses the eschatological correlative to stress the same point: Christ's resurrection is in direct contrast to death; Adam and Christ are opposites. Paul is consistent in his use of the eschatological correlative and uses it only in a very definite christological context, the comparison of Christ to a specific Old Testament figure. The judgmental dimension of the correlative in Q now has a more positive and more limited application. The context is still christology, but the specifics of that christology have been modified.

The results of this survey would indicate that an eschatological correlative does exist, that its first appearance is in the Q material and that it has been used in various ways in other theological traditions to express a variety of christological beliefs.

It is necessary at this point to stress the significance of a *Gattung* in form-critical analysis. If we accept the assumption that the New Testament is the result of the work of the community which existed after Easter, then we must give due regard to the importance of a formal structure. Once a form is located, its formal character would point to its significance in whatever levels of the tradition it is found. The mere fact of its structural formality, i.e. that it retains a constant shape, would indicate that it was important and useful for an early community. Once this significance is recognized, we can begin to look for an appropriate *Sitz im Leben der alten Kirche*, assuming that the origin of a form lies in some specific activity of the pre-literary community.

The 'sentences of holy law' investigated by Ernst Käsemann

afford an excellent example not only of the significance of a form but also of the form of one of the future Son of Man sayings in Q which is not an eschatological correlative (Luke 12.8 and par.). The 'sentences of holy law', or 'eschatological judgment pronouncement' sayings are composed of two parts 'with the same verb in each part, in the first part referring to the activity of man and in the second to the eschatological activity of God',[107] usually by putting the verb in the passive voice. The widespread use of this form in the New Testament is an indication of the importance it had in the early community. For our purpose the most important aspect of it is, of course, the occurrence of the Son of Man title in the second half of this form in Luke 12.8 and Mark 8.38.

There are two points to be made about the 'sentences of holy law' in relation to our concerns. First, their structural or formal characteristics are quite stable, though there is a development of a double form of the saying. The content of the form can and does change, while the external features of the form do not. Secondly, the context and character of the form are definitely that of judgment: eschatological judgment. The judgmental activity of the early church was expressed in this form and promised as the future work of God. Käsemann has argued that the most natural *Sitz im Leben der alten Kirche* is the celebration of the eucharist.[108] It is here that the anathema formula was located by Lietzmann and Bornkamm. Käsemann envisions a similar setting for the judgmental activity of the church represented by the 'sentences of holy law'.

The eschatological correlative in Q and in the single occurrence in Matthew is employed as a warning to the 'present' generation. It compares the coming of the Son of Man with the judgment which fell upon the contemporaries of Noah, Lot and Jonah; it warns of the coming of the Son of Man which is as universal and unexpected as a flash of lightning. In every case, the coming of the Son of Man is proclaimed because of the judgment to be expected on his arrival. It is for this reason that I would suggest that the most likely *Sitz im Leben* for the eschatological correlative would also be in the celebration of the eucharist. The 'sentences of holy law' and the eschatological correlative are used for quite similar purposes. Both are definitely aspects of the judgmental activity of the church.

[107] Perrin, *Rediscovering*, p. 22.    [108] Käsemann, 'Sentences', pp. 69f.

Although the 'sentences' and the eschatological correlative are similar in many ways, there is one important difference. The sentences are rather far removed from the Son of Man tradition. They have been used with a variety of references in the second half of the form, in only two cases with the *Son of Man*.[109] Where it occurs, Son of Man is used in the 'sentences' because it is part of a general judgment tradition. It is clear that judgment is God's activity when the form first develops. The eschatological correlative, however, is part of the future Son of Man tradition. It is a judgment form which developed to express the specific content of the Q community's understanding of the future Son of Man. Rather than adopt an already existing form, the eschatological correlative was created by the Q community to express its particular theological understanding of the Son of Man who is to come.

This conclusion becomes more certain when we compare the theological intent of the Q material with the eschatological correlative. Following the basic lines laid down by Tödt in his redaction-critical work on Q,[110] and taking into consideration the discussion above,[111] it is clear that the primary interest of the Q community was to proclaim the coming of the kingdom of God because of its assumption that the Jesus who had taught while on earth was the one who would come in the future as the Son of Man. The community's primary intent was not to proclaim the death and resurrection of Jesus, but to prepare this generation for the imminent coming of the kingdom and the appearance of Jesus as the Son of Man. Salvation lay in being a follower of Jesus, in being his disciple, and hence in being properly prepared for the apocalyptic events of the near future. The resurrection is pre-supposed by this group and it is the basis for its 'christological cognition', identifying Jesus with the coming Son of Man. Because Jesus and the coming Son of Man are one and the same, it is necessary for this group to proclaim the message which Jesus proclaimed in order that all who heed might be prepared for his coming.

Thus it is in this highly eschatologically-oriented community that we might expect the development of a form which would

---

[109] Perrin, 'Son of Man', pp. 6f.
[110] Tödt, *Son of Man*, pp. 246–69.
[111] Cf. analysis of Q in this chapter.

express the judgment of the Son of Man on those who do not prepare for his coming, i.e. for those who have not become disciples.

The occurrence of this form in Q, with its direct connection with the future Son of Man, is of major importance in determining the theological outlook of Q. The 'sentences' are used by Q, but do not originate there; it is quite the opposite with the eschatological correlative. The occurrence of this form indicates that we have a specific Q community creation which points directly toward the concerns and interests of that community.

Concisely put, the eschatological correlative demonstrates the overarching significance of the future Son of Man, as Tödt had already suggested, but it also makes clear that Tödt is wrong in asserting the authenticity of those sayings.[112] Rather, it is the eschatological correlative form which shows that the Q community's christological cognition lies in the application of the title Son of Man to Jesus. Although it is quite likely that the origin of the application of Son of Man to Jesus lies behind the Q document, this form points to the crucial nature of this concept in the Q community.

The impact of the correlative is its bringing together of the past, present and future. The Son of Man is one who will appear in the future to bring God's judgment; but that imminent appearance can be anticipated, or its character can be anticipated, by a series of past or present events which will then demand action in the present. The judgment visited upon the contemporaries of Noah, Lot and Jonah, and the universality and unexpectedness of the lightning, demand an immediate concern on the part of those who can understand, if they are to be prepared for that coming. It is the highly expectant attitude of this community which is foreign to us and which has caused trouble for interpreters. The future verb in the apodosis of the correlative has led many astray. It is not a matter of a simple present or future[113] but a collapsing of past, present and future into one moment. The correlative is an excellent grammatical form for expressing this idea.

We must notice, then, the significance of the modifications which have occurred in the Sign of Jonah explanations (Luke

---

112 Tödt, *Son of Man,* pp. 57, 112, etc.

113 Jeremias, *"Ιωνᾶς'*, p. 410, argues that the future verb demands that the saying refers to the parousia. Vielhauer, 'Jesus und der Menschensohn', p. 152, argues that the future verb used by Q indicates that the saying has a present reference.

11.30 = Matt. 12.40). There can be no doubt that this is an eschatological correlative. Both Matthew and Luke exhibit a common form – it is the content of that sentence which they have changed: For as Jonah was . . . , so the Son of Man will be . . . If we accept the fact of the correlative in Q at this point, we have moved beyond the admonitory use to which the eschatological correlative is applied in Luke 17.24ff. In the Sign of Jonah saying and explanation, the Q community is adapting a previous 'warning' form and using it to explain the refusal to give a sign. The use of the correlative is being expanded or modified; the pattern of thought which it expresses is being used to answer a question, or deal with a unit of tradition, which the Q community understands in a way quite different from that of Mark.

The Q community is interested not in the testing of Jesus or in the hiddenness of the Messiah, but in coming to grips with the fact that it understands the resurrection of Jesus as *the* sign which is now of crucial significance in bringing people into the renewed fellowship of the coming Son of Man. Thus, the Sign of Jonah passage in Q is the result of a unit of inherited tradition being supplemented by the eschatological correlative in order that the Q theology might make explicit its understanding of the refusal. The refusal is qualified: 'no sign, except the sign of Jonah'.

In chapter III the origins of this exception will be detailed. Since the Q community is adopting and using traditional material, we can expect that what its members have accepted is acceptable to them as such, or with the proper adaptations. The Sign of Jonah affords us insight into this process. The saying refusing a sign is primarily a warning against this generation or the contemporaries of the Q community. The same is the case with the following double saying (Luke 11.31f. and par.); Jonah and Solomon are great men of Israel to whom certain Gentiles responded with more certainty and forthrightness than any Israelite. Now something greater than either Jonah or Solomon is here, but this generation is just as perverse because even now they do not respond. The juxtaposing of these units is the result of the Q community's concern with the lack of response of this generation, that is, the Jews.

But once this combination has occurred, the importance of the warning theme could be modified to allow the question about the refusal of a sign to be raised. Is there a contradiction between the refusal and the double saying? It could be argued that the double saying implies that a sign has been given; perhaps not of the style requested, but nevertheless a sign. If Jesus is now recognized as the coming Son of Man, then he has indeed given a sign to his community of followers, that is, the renewed fellowship based upon his assumption to the right hand of God.

Thus, the 'exception clause' illustrates the new understanding of sign and of Jesus which has occurred in the Q community in contrast to the absolute refusal which it inherited and which is reported in Mark. But why a Sign of Jonah?

First of all, because Jonah is already present in the mind of the community because of his mention in the double saying. But secondly, and more important, Jonah and not Solomon carries with him the two or three elements which the Q community must deal with: resurrection, preaching and judgment. Jonah is the one who escapes death and is raised by God to become the preacher to the Gentiles. Jonah is the one who preaches judgment and warning to the Ninevites, who demands that they prepare for an imminent judgment. Jonah is the one who is vindicated by God, both before and after his work as a preacher of warning and repentance – in his salvation from the fish and in the great success of his word.

The Q community, then, seeks to make this comparison of Jonah and the Son of Man explicit and uses a form already at hand, the eschatological correlative. But now, rather than merely expressing a warning about the future as in Luke 17.24ff., the form serves *also* to explain how it is that Jonah is also a sign of the Son of Man. The really big change in the correlative is the addition of the word *sign* in the protasis: as Jonah was a *sign* . . . The eschatological correlative was originally used to correlate the *days* or *appearance* of the Son of Man with the days or appearance of Noah, Lot or the lightning. However, in the Jonah correlative there is now a correlation of Jonah *as a sign* with the coming of the Son of Man. The impact of the context on the eschatological correlative is obvious; a crucial change has occurred.[114]

Despite the shift in meaning, the eschatological correlative form still minimally serves the function required. The future of the Son of Man is not distinct from the past (Jonah) and is of vital concern for the present, for this generation.

[114] This will be developed further in ch. III, below.

The recognition of this form in Q not only clarifies the great significance of the Q community's theological stance but it also causes us to reconsider the origin of the Son of Man material in Q. Of the six future Son of Man sayings, three are eschatological correlatives which both Matthew and Luke place together and in the same context (Luke 17.24ff. and par.). A fourth eschatological correlative, as an explanation of the Sign of Jonah, has the effect of emphasizing the present activity of the Son of Man even though it retains the future verb. The fifth and sixth sayings are examples of the insertion of the Son of Man title into a specific form which did not originally contain a reference to the Son of Man – or the insertion of the Son of Man title into a general parable which also existed independently.

The only conclusion which can be drawn from this evidence is that the eschatological correlative is a form which comes into being in the Q community to express the Son of Man christology. Even with Q we can detect a shift of application.

## Kyrios as a Title in Q

There can be little doubt that 'Son of Man' was a very important title in the Q community. If there are indications as well that the title Son of Man is not from Jesus but represents a developing theological outlook as the delay of the parousia becomes more evident, then we might also ask about other christological titles which would also help to clarify the origins of Q's theology. The problem is even more important in the light of certain attempts to explain the origin of the Son of Man title. Is it a general title applied in Jesus' day to a transcendent, heavenly judgment figure?[115] Is it based upon the general Near-Eastern speculation about The Man?[116] Or is the title Son of Man the result of a tradition based on a *pesher* exegesis of Ps. 110.1 combined with Dan. 7.13?[117] If the latter suggestion is true, and the origin of the Son of Man christology lies in the prior use of a *Mar* christology, we would expect the title *kyrios* to be integral to the Q material. *Maranatha* does not appear in Q, but *kyrios* does occur twelve times in the following passages:

[115] Tödt, *Son of Man,* pp. 22–31. Cf. Tödt's bibliography.
[116] F. H. Borsch, *The Son of Man in Myth and History* (1967).
[117] Perrin, *Rediscovering,* pp. 164–85.

|     | *Luke*    | *Matthew*  |                                                                                                  |
|-----|-----------|------------|--------------------------------------------------------------------------------------------------|
| 1.  | 4.8       | 4.10       | Quotation of Deuteronomy 6.13. Refers to God.                                                     |
| 2.  | 4.12      | 4.7        | Quotation of Deuteronomy 6.16. Refers to God.                                                     |
| 3.  | 6.46      | 7.21       | 'Why do you call me Lord, Lord?                                                                   |
| 4.  | 7.6       | 8.8        | 'Lord, do not trouble yourself.'                                                                  |
| 5.  | 9.59      | 8.21       | 'Lord, let me first go and bury my father.'                                                       |
| 6.  | 10.2      | 9.38       | 'Pray to the Lord of the Harvest.'                                                                |
| 7.  | 10.21     | 11.25      | God, as Lord of heaven and earth.                                                                 |
| 8.  | 12.42–46  | 24.45–51   | (Lord refers to the Master in the parable of the delayed return of the Master.)                  |
| 9.  | 13.25     | 7.22       | (Lord refers to householder.)                                                                     |
| 10. | 13.35     | 23.39      | Quotation from Ps. 118.26.                                                                        |
| 11. | 16.13     | 6.24       | (Lord refers to God and Mammon.)                                                                  |
| 12. | 19.16–27  | 25.20      | (Lord refers to Master in a parable.)                                                             |

Because we are interested in the theology of the Q community, this material is best divided into five basic groups – each illustrating a different use of the title.

1. Passages 1, 2 and 10 are quotations from the Old Testament where God is referred to as Lord. This use of *kyrios* we would expect to find in any early tradition. However, 10, the quotation from Ps. 118.26, is used to describe the parousia, or at least the coming of Jesus; Jesus is the one who comes in the name of the Lord.[118] This entire saying equates Jesus with the one who is to come, the one who will be seen again, and thus implies that the earthly Jesus is identical with the coming one.

2. There are three more passages where the title *kyrios* refers to God, though not in a quotation: 6, 7 and 11. Passage 6 (Luke 10.2 and par.) refers to the *eschaton*: Pray the Lord of the harvest to send out labourers into his harvest. Discipleship and the *eschaton* are both aspects of this saying and it is the Lord who is expected to assist in the final judgment. 7 (Luke 10.21 and par.) is part of the Johannine-like statement in which Jesus praises the Father,

[118] Tödt, *Son of Man,* pp. 83, 267f.

the Lord of heaven and earth, because of what he has revealed through Jesus. At this point, the future element is gone and the present authority of Jesus as Son of God is emphasized. In 11 (Luke 16.13 and par.) *kyrios* refers to God and Mammon: 'No servant can serve two Lords, . . . You cannot serve God and Mammon.' The preparation of the disciple must be defined in terms of love toward God, of a single-minded devotion to the Lord.

3. The future coming of the Lord, or his agent, is clearly the concern of two sayings: 8 and 10. In 8 (Luke 12.42–48 and par.) is a collection of material about the coming of the Lord (and Son of Man), the time of whose return is unknown. The servants are either prepared or unprepared for the delayed appearance of the Lord. The situation described is again a combination of warning about the unexpectedness of the return and the way in which the time before the coming is to be spent. There is really no way to separate discipleship and the theme of the coming. This is especially significant when the titles Son of Man and Lord are juxtaposed as readily as they are here. That the *Maranatha* theme lies behind this correlation of the Lord and the coming seems beyond doubt; and the mention of the Son of Man within this same context would point quite strongly to the possibility that Son of Man arises in, or is at least integral to, this way of thinking about Jesus.

Passage 9 (Luke 13.25 and par.) is the other saying which emphasizes the future appearance and coming. This passage was mentioned above as a quotation from Ps. 118.26. The title *kyrios* is one which is ascribed to God, but the point is that there is one who will be coming in the Lord's name, with an explicit reference to Jesus as the one who is to come. There are overtones of passion christology in the entire context, a fact which Tödt has not recognized,[119] but we are still in the milieu of the expectation of the imminent appearance of the judge.

4. Five of these sayings can be described as dealing with discipleship: 3, 5, 9, 11 and 12.

Passage 3 (Luke 6.46 and par.) reports that some followers of Jesus have been addressing Jesus as Lord and yet not doing or following his words (Matthew: the will of the Father). The disciples, who address Jesus as Lord, are required to follow the message which he proclaimed; the follower must act as though he

[119] *Ibid.*, p. 267.

really stakes his life on the fact that Jesus is Lord. Discipleship is an active response to Jesus which will affect the entire being of the person who is truly a follower. Matthew has placed it in the context of the final judgment, as well. Thus, Lord, as a title, is understood in terms of following or keeping the sayings of Jesus.

Passage 5 (Luke 9.59 and par.) is very similar: 'Lord, let me first go and bury my father' (cf. Luke 9.61). Here the context is obvious – this request is in response to the demand 'Follow me'. And as with saying 8, this saying follows immediately upon a Son of Man saying. The point being made is one about the heavy demands placed upon those who follow. The disciple cannot expect to be a part-time follower but must be willing to commit himself in a complete way, similar to the demand made upon the servants who must watch for the return of their Lord. There must be a single-mindedness on the part of those who are truly disciples. Son of Man and Lord both seem to be defined by a description of what is demanded of disciples.

Passage 9 (Luke 13.25 and par.) is part of an answer to the disciples who have asked about the paucity of those who will be saved. The householder has shut the door; those who knock address him as Lord. They are rejected because, although they have been with him, they are described as workers of iniquity. Only those who are willing to *act* as though Jesus is Lord, will be able to enter the heavenly table fellowship.

Passage 11 uses the word Lord as a reference for God, but the context is definitely discipleship once more. The singleness of purpose that is required, the serving of only one master, is the way one indicates that God is Lord.

Passage 12 (Luke 19.16–27 and par.) is the parable of the talents in which the householder is addressed as Lord. A secondary theme, which Luke emphasizes with his introductory comment, is the delay of the coming of the Lord. The point of the parable is a criticism of those disciples who do not put to use the gifts they received. The forgiveness which is a part of the life of the disciple must be appropriated and put into action if one is to be a true disciple. The Lord is also the judge. When he comes, all will be assessed.

5. Finally, there are two sayings which stress the authority of the Lord. The first is 4 (Luke 7.6 and par.) in which the centurion of Capernaum addresses Jesus as Lord and implies that Jesus'

authority is clearly visible to one who has authority. This is the only time where the word appears in Q, and even here it is not directly applied to Jesus. It is also interesting to note that the context is Jesus' healing power, not his authority as teacher. It may be that this is a preliminary hint of the development of the concept of Jesus as the one with authority which is fully developed in Mark. But the discipleship idea is not far removed; the centurion is a model of the disciple because he acts upon his recognition of Jesus' authority.

Passage 7 (Luke 10.21 and par.) uses *kyrios* to refer to God as the Lord of heaven and earth (see above). The context is the authority which the Father has given to the Son. The Father cannot be known except 'by the Son'. The Son has the authority to reveal these things to whomsoever he may choose. As in the previous saying, we may have here the beginning of a Son of God christology in the Q community, developing out of the authority which it ascribes to Jesus. Or is it the other way around; has the Son of God title led to the ascription of authority to Jesus?

In summary, the word *kyrios* does appear in the early Palestinian material and is used a number of times directly of Jesus, not just in quotations referring to God. But the context is varied; the majority of the sayings relate to the problem of discipleship. If *kyrios* were used in a non-christological sense, we would expect to find *Rabbi* and *didaskalos* in Q, but *Rabbi* does not occur at all and 'teacher' occurs only once, in Luke 6.40 and par., where the teacher is said to be greater than the student. Thus there seems to be corroborating evidence for the origin of *kyrios* in Q in the Aramaic *Maranatha* – aside from the linguistic and *pesher* evidence.[120] It is certainly further evidence against the *religionsgeschichtliche Schule's* argument about the late Hellenistic origin of *kyrios*.[121]

## Redaction Analysis

For the purpose of this thesis I have chosen to use the word 'redaction' to refer to that type of criticism which seeks to understand the theological motivation of the editor-author by a careful analysis of the specific changes which he has made in the tradition he has received. To be distinguished from redaction criticism is

---

[120] Cf. Perrin, *Rediscovering*, pp. 164–85.
[121] Wilhelm Bousset, *Kyrios Christos* (3rd ed., 1926), pp. 75–104.

composition analysis which focuses attention on the arrangement of the units and the over-all structure of a work.

The difficulty in using either of these methods in an investigation of Q should be obvious. Q represents, first of all, an early stage of tradition and the isolation of earlier material to compare with the Q redaction is not a simple task. Secondly, the order of Q is not an established fact, nor is it likely to be, as is the order of Matthew and Luke. Q must be reconstructed from its occurrence in the gospels. Even if we can reach some agreement about the order of Q, we still have no certainty about the completeness of our reconstruction; both Matthew and Luke may have omitted some sections, or may have included parts of Q which the other editor has neglected.

Nevertheless, there are certain established factors which we can assume to be of significance and which act as correlatives when a series of conclusions are eventually compared. The work of Tödt, which was described above, operates from the established common material of Matthew and Luke and proceeds to seek a theological theme which would explain the peculiarities of the material; e.g. the lack of any passion material, the almost exclusive interest in the sayings of Jesus, and the relation of present and future Son of Man sayings. Käsemann has assisted in defining the nature of the Son of Man material by describing the extent as well as the nature of the 'eschatological judgment pronouncement' sayings. The isolation of the eschatological correlative as a form particular to the Q material has also added some insight to the theological *Sitz im Leben* of the Q community and of a possible development or change in their understanding of its significance.

However, redaction criticism is best illustrated in the history of the tradition of the Sign of Jonah presented in the following chapter. We shall be able to see the specific modification and addition of material to an earlier saying refusing a sign. We shall have specific facts to deal with and it will enable us to look closely at the motives behind any redactional activity. The obvious issue raised is the possibility of other pericopes which will allow us to see the Q community at work in accepting and modifying tradition.

The following three units fit the requirements for such a task. They are clearly from the Q stratum of tradition but are related to the tradition in Mark. As in the Sign of Jonah, we have a situation where we might be able to see additions or modifications of specific material to which Mark is an independent witness. This does not mean, of course, that Mark is chronologically prior to Q; the opposite is more likely the case. But it does mean that Mark may have preserved a tradition which either was more primitive or was common to both. Undoubtedly, it is difficult to tell where or when Mark or Q has been at work in modifying the earlier tradition. But we can clarify the distinction that exists between Mark and Q and we may find specific redaction. At least this is the question which must now be asked.

The following three units are possible source of redactional evidence for the theology of Q:

1. Luke 11.14–23 = Matt. 12.22–30 = Mark 3.22–27: the Beelzebul accusation.
2. Luke 11.33(34–36) = Matt. 5.15 = Mark 4.21: a saying concerning light.
3. Luke 12.8–12 = Matt. 12.31f. = Mark 3.28–30: the sin against the Holy Spirit.

*The Beelzebul Accusation*  The first thing to note is the apparent doublet in Matt. 9.32–34. As far as the specific accusation is concerned, it is of little significance because the reference to the Prince of Demons seems to be merely a carry-over from Matt. 12.24. In a sense, Matthew is indicating the nature of the response of some of those who witness the healing and is also anticipating the full-fledged controversy which he rejects in ch. 12. There is no Markan parallel for 9.32–34, and we must assume that Matthew has included this healing at this point for his own purposes.

The limits and extent of Q and Mark in this pericope are not difficult to define. Matthew and Luke agree in introducing the accusation with a healing story while Mark explains the accusation by reporting that Jesus' friends went out to seize him saying, 'He is beside himself.' It is not clear just what it is that causes Jesus' friends to make this comment; the two preceding units in Mark both mention the casting out of demons, first in 3.11 in a very general report, and secondly in the call of the disciples (3.13–15) where Jesus gives them authority to cast out demons. At any rate, the accusation in Mark is that Jesus is possessed of a demon, whereas in Q Jesus is accused of being in league with Beelzebul because of a specific healing miracle.

The actual accusation in Luke 11.15 and par. is quite similar in all three gospels and could be the result of Matthew and Luke using Mark, or a stable tradition behind all three reports. The next clear indication of Q is in Luke 11.19f. and par.: 'If I cast out demons by Beelzebul, by whom do your sons cast them out? Therefore they shall be your judges. But if I, by the finger [Matthew: Spirit] of God cast out demons, then the kingdom of God has come upon you.' Following this statement, Matthew and Luke pick up Mark again and, with much verbal agreement between Matthew and Mark but not with Luke, relate the story of the strong man overcome by a stronger. Q finishes the incident with the words (Luke 11.23 and par.): 'He who is not with me is against me, and he who does not gather with me, scatters.'

There can be little doubt that we have here a tradition about a Beelzebul accusation which existed in Mark and Q but with significant differences. What do the Q variants tell us about the theology of the Q community?

The conclusion of the Q version (Luke 11.23 and par.) definitely emphasizes the importance of discipleship, of following Jesus. By attaching it to this incident, the nature of discipleship is defined by the Q community as recognizing the significance of the authority of Jesus. The message of the kingdom of God has been validated by the exorcisms; but this is not an unambiguous sign. The man who could not speak, now does speak. The contemporaries of Jesus could not accept this as an indication of the importance of Jesus; they do not listen to the words which proclaim the kingdom of God.

When the general conclusion is then seen in relation to the Q addition (Luke 11.19f. and par.), we see that this kingdom of God saying is really the main point of this whole incident for Q. The true disciple prepares for the coming of the kingdom of God by recognizing the validity of the message of Jesus; it is a message just as relevant to the Q community as it was in Jesus' own day. It is likely that the early church was engaged in exorcism and was accused of being in league with Beelzebul and that the Q story is an attempt to define the disciple as one who participates in the fellowship of those who rely on Jesus.

Mark seems to be more interested in defining the nature of Jesus – his is a christological statement, and not primarily a definition of discipleship. Jesus is not a split personality but is clearly the one fully in power of himself and of the 'strong man', Beelzebul. The division is not within the kingdom of God *nor* in the kingdom of Satan, but exists between the two.

*A Saying concerning Light*  In this parable about light we have an apparent use of Mark by Matthew and Luke with the addition of a further saying about the eye. As Bultmann suggests, it may be that the Q expansion is actually independent of the parable about the lamp.[122] The possibility is increased by the fact that Matthew places the Q saying (6.22f.) in another part of the Sermon on the Mount, away from 5.15.

The problem here is the lack of an interconnection between the two sayings, and we therefore cannot use the Q material as evidence of an expansion of the saying preserved in Mark; it is possible, but not clear enough. It does give us some indication of Luke's activity in combining them, or Matthew's in separating them. However, this pericope is of no help in locating the Q community's *redaction*.

*The Sin against the Holy Spirit*  The interpretation of this passage has been made unnecessarily difficult because of a misreading of Mark 3.28. Manson assumed that the words in 3.28 τοῖς υἱοῖς τῶν ἀνθρώ πων are meant to be a parallel to the prepositional phrase in 3.29, εἰς τὸ πνεῦμα τὸ ἅγιον, i.e. that the sins and blasphemies forgiven in 3.28 are sins *against* the sons of men (dative of respect) to be contrasted with the unforgivable sin of blasphemy against (εἰς) the Holy Spirit.[123] This interpretation causes problems for Manson because he must now try to explain what it means to blaspheme against the sons of men; he decides that this would be blaspheming against the disciples, before the Holy Spirit has begun to work in them. The Q saying is less original for Manson because the blasphemies against the Son of Man are forgiven. Since this is just the opposite of the previous statement in Luke (12.8f.), Manson argues that ὁ υἱὸς τοῦ ἀνθρώπου should have originally meant merely 'a man', i.e. should be understood in the generic sense. The movement from Aramaic (Q) to Greek has caused all the trouble. All this is based upon the judgment that Mark and Q are independent!

Tödt objects to Manson's analysis 'if only for reasons of

---

[122] Bultmann, *History*, p. 87.    [123] Manson, *Sayings*, pp. 109f.

method'.[124] Manson is accused of removing Luke 12.10 and par. from the context of Q and trying to see it in relation to Luke 12.8f. Tödt sees 12.8f. connected to 12.10 because of a secondary, catchword relation (Son of Man). If we put Luke 12.10 in the context of the Beelzebul opposition, the implication is that Son of Man, for Q, is a reference to the earthly activity of the Son of Man, and that in the situation after Easter blasphemy against the one in whom the Spirit is now working cannot be forgiven. Thus Q assumes that there are two periods in the history of salvation; those who do not follow the earthly Jesus will be forgiven, while those who deny the risen Son of Man will not be forgiven.

Mark's version must be later than Q's, says Tödt, because he does not make the distinction between the Spirit's activity before and after the resurrection.[125] The victory over the demons would demand that the Spirit be active in Jesus during his ministry. 'Mark or a predecessor' may have known the Q saying but would have considered it to be offensive since it implies that blasphemy against the sovereign Son of Man is to be forgiven.[126]

In Excursus IV, Tödt comments on Wellhausen's analysis of this pericope.[127] He is critical of Wellhausen for judging Mark's version to be earlier than Q's, he seems to assume that Mark 3.28 is not clear and that the 'recipients and contents of the blasphemies are no longer distinguishable. So the meaning of the saying has become obscure.'[128] Rather, says Tödt, Mark has redacted the Q-type saying because he does not want to use Son of Man (singular) to refer to the earthly ministry of Jesus.

In contrast to Tödt, a comparison of the synoptic material would indicate that Mark's version of the saying is earlier. First of all, it is quite likely that a saying claiming that all sins can be forgiven, except the sin of speaking against the Holy Spirit, could have been a part of the pre-Markan tradition. The phrase τοῖς υἱοῖς τῶν ἀνθρώπων could have been an Aramaic expression to refer to men. What reason Mark might have had for changing a singular to a plural is hard to discover. The saying could have existed without any use of the word βλασφημία; Tödt shows that this word is part of the vocabulary of the early church. The Semitic phrase 'to speak against' has been simplified by using βλασφημία in its

---

[124] Tödt, *Son of Man*, p. 118.    [125] *Ibid.*, pp. 119f.
[126] *Ibid.*, p. 120.    [127] *Ibid.*, pp. 312–18.    [128] *Ibid.*, p. 315.

place. Matthew finds no difficulty in retaining the dative τοῖς ἀνθρώποις in 12.31, i.e., he drops the τοῖς υἱοῖς of Mark.

The Q saying is an expansion of the primitive Markan-type saying and changes the generic 'sons of men' to a singular as a designation of Jesus. This modification has the effect of splitting the ministry of Jesus prior to the resurrection from the ministry of Jesus as the expected Son of Man. Mark's version is a christological statement about the continuity of the authority of Jesus, while the Q version is an apologetic statement about the possibility of forgiveness in the situation after Easter. The Jews who rejected Jesus before the resurrection can be forgiven and can become part of the table fellowship of those who await the coming of the kingdom of God. Mark is concerned with those who are now under the duress of denying the faith in the light of persecution. The concluding statement in Mark 3.30, 'Because they said, He has an evil spirit', is Mark's attempt to create a connecting link with the previous pericope and to develop the theme of denial. Q, on the other hand, stresses the openness of the fellowship and invites those who are outside to join.

Thus we have in this pericope an example of the Q community's redaction: they have recast a reference to 'sons of men' into a statement about their recognition of the change of outlook toward, and soteriological significance of, the resurrection. A denial after the resurrection is a denial of the Holy Spirit but before the resurrection it is merely a misunderstanding of the importance of Jesus. 'This generation' has failed to see; a continuation of this near-sightedness will bring disaster upon them.

## The Order of Q

As I have already indicated, it is of some importance that we be relatively certain about the order or arrangement of Q. Whether this order has been inherited or not, it is accepted or created by the Q community and would help to illuminate the redactional hints we have already found. But Q is a reconstructed entity and we cannot proceed along lines as definite as we might with Mark, Matthew, or Luke. However, if there is some way to come to some conclusion about a general arrangement of Q, we can at least begin to ask questions about the proximity of certain pericopes, or of the meaning of certain apparent collections of material.

Manson set the stage for these questions, as Tödt has made clear.[129] First, Manson pointed to the Lukan practice of using documents in blocks rather than conflating them as Matthew does. Therefore we might expect that Luke's order of Q material is closer to that of his source. Secondly, Manson noticed that the arrangement of M corresponds at four points with the arrangement of Q, in Luke's order.[130]

| *Q* | *M* |
|---|---|
| 1. John's preaching | |
| 2. The temptations | |
| 3. Jesus' preaching | 1. Jesus' preaching |
| 4. Centurion of Capernaum | |
| 5. Jesus and John the Baptist | |
| 6. Mission charge | 2. Mission charge |
| 7. Beelzebul | |
| 8. Refusal of a sign | |
| | 3. Parables of missionary work |
| | 4. Nature of the Christian fellowship |
| | 5. Conditions of service and reward (cf. Q 10) |
| | 6. The refusers (cf. Q 11) |
| 9. Against Pharisees | 7. Against Pharisees |
| 10. Service, sacrifice, reward (cf. M 5) | |
| 11. Refusers (cf. M 6) | |
| 12. Eschatology | 8. Eschatology |

Beyond this parallelism, there are further parallels within 'Jesus' preaching' and the 'Mission charge'. Manson is understandably hesitant to make too much of these parallels but suggests they they indicate that a 'rough outline of the essentials of the teaching (existed) at an earlier stage of the tradition than is represented by Q or M'.[131] In the bulk of *The Sayings of Jesus* Manson

129 Manson, *Sayings,* pp. 21f.; Tödt, *Son of Man,* p. 242.
130 The following table is from Manson, *Sayings,* p. 21.
131 Manson, *Sayings,* p. 23.

follows the order of Q in Luke and seems to be convinced that he has reached some solid ground.

V. Taylor takes up the work of Manson and asks if there can be any further way of showing the accuracy of the Lukan order.[132] His method is based upon the accepted analysis of the editorial activities or Matthew. Since Matthew is the one who conflates, is it possible to show that he has used Q as a supplement to the other sayings source, M? Taylor takes Matthew section by section and puts the Q material in each section in the Lukan order. For example, all the Q material in the Sermon on the Mount is set down in one column in the Lukan order, and the corresponding Lukan sayings are noted in the second column. The result is a high level of agreement in order. Where the order is not similar, Taylor finds that it is possible to find editorial reasons, on the part of Matthew or Luke, for the specific change noted. Thus Matthew has apparently used Q as a source of the sayings of Jesus to supplement a source which is partially similar, that is, M. Previous indications of the editorial methods of Matthew and Luke are found to be corroborated by the Q material as well. Matthew's special material seems to be more important for him when M and Q contain similar material.

Taylor concludes that Q must now be considered a document. However, of more importance for us is that Matthew was freely creative in his use of the tradition, at least in respect to its order. Taylor calls for a further examination of M; in effect, a redactional study of Matthew seeking to make sense of the 'framework' or, to put it in source-critical terms, the material peculiar to Matthew. But Q, whether a document or not, was in a stable enough condition to be arranged and, for the most part, the order of Q in Luke is a good indication of the original order of Q. With this in mind, we can cautiously use the arrangement of Q as an indication of the theology of the community, if there are other indications from the material that this might be possible.

[132] Vincent Taylor, 'The original Order of Q', in A. J. B. Higgins, ed.; *New Testament Essays: Studies in Memory of T. W. Manson* (1959), pp. 246–69.

# III

## THE HISTORY OF THE TRADITION
## OF THE SIGN OF JONAH

### INTRODUCTION AND PRELIMINARY RÉSUMÉ

WE NOW turn to a direct consideration of the Sign of Jonah. The survey of research on this problem indicated that the impasse could be surmounted by combining a form-critical analysis with the insights of redaction criticism. In chapter II the nature and character of redaction criticism was set forth, with special emphasis on the theology of Q because of its comparative neglect and also in anticipation of the results of the investigation of the history of the tradition of the Sign of Jonah. The purpose of this final section of the thesis is to apply the method suggested: the combination of a form-critical history of the tradition with a careful consideration of the theological tendencies of the various levels in the tradition. The result is a unified understanding of the role played by the theology of each redactor, and a clarification of the origin of the text as it has been handed down to us. The Sign of Jonah is not a stable, simple idea which is passed on intact, but rather is one of the many phrases or concepts used by the early church in coming to grips with the faith it proclaimed. The careful scrutiny of this one complicated pericope can thus open up new insights into the complex phenomena of New Testament theology.

The argument of the following sections attempts to show that the Markan version of the story of the refusal of a sign reflects an early tradition about the evil character of this generation and its misunderstanding of the early church's use of the 'signs' or wonders that have been reported about Jesus. This early tradition about the seeking and refusal of a sign was also part of the tradition received by the Q community, and it is in this community that the specific reference to a Sign of Jonah first appears. The origin of this saying is to be found in the particular juxtaposition of certain apologetic traditions which are directed against this generation. The precise wording of the Q version of the explanation of the Sign of Jonah is not recoverable, but the outline of the eschatological correlative, which does remain, allows us to reconstruct its probable form.

Luke's version of the saying appears to be closer to the Q version, and yet his arrangement of the material also suggests that he has understood Q in a slightly new way. Matthew, on the other hand, has used a characteristic quotation to clarify his further reinterpretation of the significance of the Sign of Jonah. At each stage, the insights of redaction criticism will be utilized to substantiate the results of the form-critical analysis.

Any attempt to reconstruct the history of the tradition of synoptic material must begin with the results of source criticism. The 'assured result' of the literary comparison of the three synoptics is the priority of Mark as a literary source for Matthew and Luke, and the use of Q by Matthew and Luke.[1] Recent attempts to overturn the two-document hypothesis have as yet produced minimal evidence to warrant our rejection of the basic essentials of this solution.[2] We will assume that Matthew and Luke rely on Mark and Q as well as upon some other material peculiar to each of them. However, it is not necessary to presuppose that they are mere collectors and organizers of already formed or even written tradition. Rather, we shall have to be alert for their large and small changes or modifications in what they received. In other words, although we accept the basic outlines of the two-document hypothesis, form criticism has demanded that we consider the tradition and the writer to be less stable or static and more open to development or change.

Any study of the history of the tradition must begin, of course, with the relevant texts as they are received and then work back from the present form toward the earlier layers. Rather than present the history in that form, I propose to assume that that work has been completed and to present the results of that work in what would now be considered the course of its growth and development; that is, rather than repeat the 'peeling' process, I will begin at the available beginning and build toward the final form of the text.

[1] Cf. Kümmel, *Introduction,* pp. 37–59, on the synoptic problem.
[2] William Farmer, *The Synoptic Problem* (1964), is the latest statement of this position.

To assist in clarifying the following argument, I have inserted at this point the following reconstructed texts, along with the terminology which I will use when referring to them.

The Markan *sign-refusal saying* (Mark 8.11–13) is from an early stage of the tradition:

8.11. καὶ ἐξῆλθον οἱ Φαρισαῖοι καὶ ἤρξαντο συζητεῖν αὐτῷ.
ζητοῦντες παρ᾽ αὐτοῦ σημεῖον ἀπὸ τοῦ οὐρανοῦ, πειράζοντες αὐτόν.

12. καὶ ἀναστενάξας τῷ πνεύματι αὐτοῦ λέγει· τί ἡ γενεὰ αὕτη ζητεῖ
σημεῖον; ἀμὴν λέγω ὑμῖν, εἰ δοθήσεται τῇ γενεᾷ ταύτῃ σημεῖον.

13. καὶ ἀφεὶς αὐτοὺς πάλιν ἐμβὰς ἀπῆλθεν εἰς τὸ πέραν.

The Q saying which was received by Matthew and Luke was composed of the following sections:

(*a*) The *request*: specific details not clear; a σημεῖον is requested.

(*b*) The *reply* of Jesus:

> ἡ γενεὰ αὕτη γενεὰ πονηρά ἐστιν.
> σημεῖον ζητεῖ, καὶ σημεῖον οὐ δοθήσεται αὐτῇ εἰ μὴ τὸ σημεῖον
> Ἰωνᾶ.

(*c*) The *explanation*:

> καθὼς (ὥσπερ) γὰρ ἐγένετο (ἦν) Ἰωνᾶς . . . ,
> οὕτως ἔσται ὁ υἱὸς τοῦ ἀνθρώπου . . .

(*d*) The double saying, Luke 11.31f. and par.:

> βασίλισσα νότου ἐγερθήσεται ἐν τῇ κρίσει μετὰ τῆς γενεᾶς ταύτης
> καὶ κατακρινεῖ αὐτήν.
> ὅτι ἦλθεν ἐκ τῶν περάτων τῆς γῆς ἀκοῦσαι τὴν σοφίαν Σολομῶνος,
> καὶ ἰδοὺ πλεῖον Σολομῶνος ὧδε.
> ἄνδρες Νινευεῖται ἀναστήσονται ἐν τῇ κρίσει μετὰ τῆς γενεᾶς
> ταύτης
> καὶ κατακρινοῦσιν αὐτήν·
> ὅτι μετενόησαν εἰς τὸ κήρυγμα Ἰωνᾶ, καὶ ἰδοὺ πλεῖον Ἰωνᾶ ὧδε.

Matthew combines elements of Mark and Q in different ways in his double version, 12.38–42 and 16.1–4:

12.38. τότε ἀπεκρίθησαν αὐτῷ τινες τῶν γραμματέων καὶ Φαρισαίων
λέγοντες·
διδάσκαλε, θέλομεν ἀπὸ σοῦ σημεῖον ἰδεῖν.

39. ὁ δὲ ἀποκριθεὶς εἶπεν αὐτοῖς·
   γενεὰ πονηρὰ καὶ μοιχαλὶς σημεῖον ἐπιζητεῖ,
   καὶ σημεῖον οὐ δοθήσεται αὐτῇ εἰ μὴ τὸ σημεῖον Ἰωνᾶ τοῦ
   προφήτου.

40. ὥσπερ γὰρ ἦν Ἰωνᾶς ἐν τῇ κοιλίᾳ τοῦ κήτους τρεῖς ἡμέρας καὶ
   τρεῖς νύκτας,
   οὕτως ἔσται ὁ υἱὸς τοῦ ἀθρώπου ἐν τῇ καρδίᾳ τῆς γῆς τρεῖς
   ἡμέρας καὶ τρεῖς νύκτας.

41–42 (Double saying).

16.1. καὶ προσελθόντες οἱ Φαρισαῖοι καὶ Σαδδουκαῖοι πειράζοντες
   ἐπηρώτησαν αὐτὸν σημεῖον ἐκ τοῦ οὐρανοῦ ἐπιδεῖξαι αὐτοῖς.

2. ὁ δὲ ἀποκριθεὶς εἶπεν αυτοῖς·
   ὀψίας γενομένης λέγετε·
   εὐδία, πυρράζει γὰρ ὁ οὐρανός.

3. καὶ πρωΐ· σήμερον χειμών,
   πυρράζει γὰρ στυγνάζων ὁ οὐρανός.
   τὸ μὲν πρόσωπον τοῦ οὐρανοῦ γινώσκετε διακρίνειν,
   τὰ δὲ σημεῖα τῶν καιρῶν οὐ δύνασθε;

4. γενεὰ πονηρὰ καὶ μοιχαλὶς σημεῖον ἐπιζητεῖ,
   καὶ σημεῖον οὐ δοθήσεται αὐτῇ εἰ μὴ τὸ σημεῖον Ἰωνᾶ.
   καὶ καταλιπὼν αὐτοὺς ἀπῆλθεν.

Finally, Luke also knows both Mark and Q when he composes his version of the incident, 11.16, 29f., 31f.:

11.16. ἕτεροι δὲ πειράζοντες σημεῖον ἐξ οὐρανοῦ ἐζήτουν παρ' αὐτοῦ.

29. τῶν δὲ ὄχλων ἐπαθροιζομένων ἤρξατο λέγειν·
   ἡ γενεὰ αὕτη γενεὰ πονηρά ἐστιν.
   σημεῖον ζητεῖ, καὶ σημεῖον οὐ δοθήσεται αὐτῇ εἰ μὴ τὸ σημεῖον
   Ἰωνᾶ.

30. καθὼς γὰρ ἐγένετο Ἰωνᾶς
   τοῖς Νινευείταις σημεῖον,
   οὕτως ἔσται καὶ ὁ υἱὸς τοῦ ἀνθρώπου
   τῇ γενεᾷ ταύτῃ.

31–32 (Double saying).

## MARK'S USE OF THE TRADITION

### *The Distinctiveness of the Markan Refusal-saying*

We have already seen that Mark is primarily a user of traditions which he has arranged and ordered to present his statement of the kerygma. If this is correct, then we can expect to find that his report of the refusal of a sign will contain indications of an early origin and that the most revealing aspect of Mark's version will be its location within the framework of the gospel. It will be the purpose of this section to present the evidence in support of the claim that Mark's version is close to an early account of Jesus' refusal to give a sign to the Pharisees. The tradition which Mark uses also appears to form the basis of the Q version. Thus, even though we might expect the Q report to be older, it shows signs of theological development which appear to be based upon a version somewhat similar to that used by Mark.

The early Aramaic or Semitic quality of Mark's version is quite clear. Mark reports that the Pharisees ask Jesus for a sign from heaven in order to test him. Jesus' reply, in response to this demand, is in the form of a question: 'Why is it that this generation is seeking a sign? Truly I say to you, if this generation will be given a sign!' (Mark 8.12: ἀμὴν λέγω ὑμῖν, εἰ δοθήσεται τῇ γενεᾷ ταύτῃ σημεῖον). This peculiar phrase is a literal rendering of a typical Hebraic oath formula: May this or that happen to me, if such-and-such is true (or is done).[3] This formula is not Greek nor is it typically Aramaic, but probably is an archaizing Hebrew expression. The effect it has is obvious: it is a very forceful way of saying *no* within a Semitic environment. It would seem likely that Mark has here taken over a statement from his source and retained the primitive wording; it would be difficult to account for it in any other way.

It has also been suggested that an Aramaism lies behind the question: 'Why does this generation seek a sign?' (Mark 8.12b: τί ἡ γενεὰ αὕτη ζητεῖ σημεῖον;).[4] However, since this use of τί is also a standard Koine form, we cannot be certain.[5] The impact of these

---

[3] E. Kautzsch, ed., *Gesenius' Hebrew Grammar* (1910), pp. 471f. Cf. also Paul Joüon, *Grammaire de l'Hébreu biblique* (1923), p. 505.

[4] Matthew Black, *An Aramaic Approach to the Gospels and Acts* (3rd ed., 1967), p. 123.

[5] Moulton, *Grammar*, Vol. III, p. 127.

two sentences, coming in close proximity, would be especially forceful and meaningful to someone who could catch the Semitic overtones. The antiquity of the Markan report seems evident.

There are other elements in these verses which are part of the Markan framework. The specific mention of the Pharisees as those who tempt Jesus is surely Markan. Luke does not mention any specific group and Matthew seems to include with the Pharisees either the scribes (12.38) or the Sadducees (16.1). This is an awkward place for the Pharisees to appear in Mark's gospel, and it may indicate some special concern on his part to include them, or simply that it was part of his tradition. The verb ἐξῆλθον seems to indicate an inclusion, i.e., an attempt to avoid the awkwardness of the transition from 8.10. It is a typically Markan feature to portray the Pharisees in the role of opponents and to refer to Pharisees alone, not coupling them with the scribes or Sadducees.[6] Mark is putting content into the phrase 'this generation' (8.12a); the Pharisees are Jesus' true opponents in the sign-demanding situation.

Another particularly Markan characteristic is the use of the word πειράζοντες, which is copied by both Matthew (16.1) and Luke. The theme of temptation is part of Mark's christological purpose.[7] For the present, the word does seem to come into the tradition from Mark because in Matt. 12, where Matthew is more dependent upon the Q report, πειράζοντες is not used, although it does occur in Matt. 16. Related to he ttemptation theme is the explicit definition of the requested sign, that it is to be a 'sign from heaven' (σημεῖον ἀπὸ τοῦ οὐρανοῦ). As with the word πειράζοντες, Matthew does not use this phrase in ch. 12, although he does use it, and elaborates it, in ch. 16. Both Matthew and Luke use the preposition ἐκ (ἐξ) and not Mark's ἀπό.

A final and thoroughly puzzling aspect of Mark's report is the unusual phrase: καὶ ἀναστενάξας τῷ πνεύματι αὐτοῦ ('And sighing in his spirit . . .', 8.12). This is the only occurrence of this word in the New Testament, although the verb without the prefix does appear in Mark 7.34.[8] It has been suggested that it is merely a way of expressing Jesus' exasperation at the request for a sign,[9] or, on

---

[6] Mark 2.18, 24; 3.6; (7.2); 10.2.
[7] Cf. pp. 25–30 above and Best, *Temptation*, pp. 3–62.
[8] Also at II Cor. 5.2, 4; Rom. 8.23; James 5.9.
[9] Taylor, *Mark,* p. 361.

the contrary, that it may reflect certain exorcistic or magical practices.[10] The verb, as used in 7.34, does seem to indicate an exorcistic use. If so, does it indicate that Mark or his tradition conceives of the opponents of Jesus as part of the attack upon Jesus by the demons? But the narrative continues by having Jesus refuse to give the sign, *not* by exorcising the demons within the Pharisees! When the temptation theme appears elsewhere in Mark, the exorcistic overtones do not exist (10.2 and 12.15). It is quite possible that we have here a conflict between Mark and his sources. Since 8.11–13 already seems to have an early Semitic character, this phrase might also reflect the interest of that earlier tradition.

In summary we can say that this pericope in Mark does contain one explicit, linguistic, Semitic statement and possibly two others. Alongside this early material is Mark's own redactional or framework modification. Mark seems to be willing to preserve older material without a definite or complete rewriting even though there may be some internal conflict. If this is so, then the order or arrangement of Mark would more thoroughly reflect his theological tendencies.

## Composition Analysis

At the end of the incident immediately prior to the sign-refusal, the feeding of the four thousand (8.1–10), Mark reports that Jesus enters a boat with his disciples and travels to the district of Dalmanutha (or Magdala). Mark places the sign-refusal incident in Dalmanutha and then closes it with the report that Jesus left the Pharisees and went back to the other side of the lake, i.e. to Bethsaida (8.22; cf. 7.31). Two incidents are isolated geographically from the non-disciples – the sign-refusal (8.11–13) and a conversation in the boat when the disciples do not understand Jesus' reference to the leaven of the Pharisees and of Herod (8.14–21). Thus the sign incident is sandwiched between two parts of the complete account of the feeding and its interpretation. Mark's intent seems clear: the sign of the feeding of the four thousand is not understood by the Pharisees or by the disciples, although Jesus tries to interpret it for the latter. The sign was

[10] Campbell Bonner, 'Traces of Thaumaturgic Technique in the Miracles', *HTR* XX (1927), pp. 171–81.

given, but it was not a sign from heaven. Jesus does not accede to
their demands, yet he proclaims and acts the message of God for
those who perceive. The Messiah is hidden in the signs which are
not of heaven but which have been granted and which are really
an integral part of his work.

It is not only the feeding incident which is the context for this
saying. It is also the entire first section of the gospel (1.1–8.26) –
the mighty acts of Jesus. Again and again Jesus acts with power
and authority, and yet the Pharisees do not see or hear.

The major turning-point of the gospel follows almost immediately upon the special teaching which takes place in the boat
(8.14–21). Caesarea Philippi with its great confession and misunderstanding begins at 8.27.[11] The incident that completes the
first part of the gospel (8.22–26) is the story of the 'progressive'
healing of the blind man at Bethsaida. Jesus is at first unable to
heal him completely, and it is only after a second effort that his
sight is fully restored. Then follows the confession of Peter at
Caesarea Philippi. Mark, when he places this healing story at this
point in the gospel, is anticipating the limited understanding of the
disciples who as yet do not fully comprehend the mission of Jesus.
Peter's confession, that Jesus is the Christ, must be rebuked when
the full implications of this messiahship are sketched out. The
healing of the blind man serves as a turning-point in that this
healing symbolizes the partial insight that is about to occur among
the disciples, and it anticipates the final full understanding that
will occur at the death of Jesus. The healing of blind Bartimaeus
(10.46–52) serves a similar purpose for Mark at the completion of
the threefold section on teaching (8.27–10.45), when the passion
story itself is about to begin.[12] Blind Bartimaeus is more know-
ledgeable than the blind man at Bethsaida because he addresses
Jesus as Son of David in anticipation of the triumphal entry. The
centurion receives full sight when Jesus dies on the cross (15.39).

There is a further structural parallel in these two stories of
healings of blind men. At the conclusion of the healing in Bethsaida, the man now healed is sent home with the words: 'Do not
even enter the village' (Mark 8.26). The healing of Bartimaeus
concludes with the comment that Bartimaeus 'followed him on

---

[11] Cf. analysis by Perrin, *Redaction Criticism,* pp. 40–57.
[12] T. Alec Burkill, *Mysterious Revelation: An Examination of the Philosophy
of St Mark's Gospel* (1963), pp. 142, 190.

the way' (10.52). There is no reason for the blind man of Beth-saida to return to Galilee and eventually to Jerusalem, whereas Bartimaeus can now follow on the road toward the suffering and death of Jesus. Although the Galilean ministry is now completed in 8.22–26, the complete revelation of the meaning of Jesus is yet to occur. 'Do not even enter the village' is advice to a disciple who is beginning to see, while Bartimaeus's 'blind sight' is typical of the true, complete and ideal disciple: he follows in 'the way'.

The saying refusing a sign (8.11–13) thus serves the function of contrasting this generation with those who are beginning to see the character of the signs which Jesus has performed. The Jews are sightless. Jesus leaves them and turns to the disciples who are now instructed in the ways of the action of God; they are to beware of the leaven of the Pharisees and their insensitivity to the signs which have been given; or to paraphrase Dibelius: epiphanies remain a secret to the Pharisees and the Herodians.[13] The saying refusing a sign is itself almost a simple aside used by Mark to high-light his special interpretation of the feeding miracle and its anticipation of the passion. Or from another point of view, this saying sums up the apostasy of the Jews and anticipates their major role in the crucifixion.

Under these circumstances, the Semitic and rough character of Mark's version of the sign-seeking saying can be understood as a lack of concern on Mark's part to spend much time rewriting it. It serves an essentially minor purpose, even though it could be seen as a kind of summary of the Jewish attitude toward Jesus (cf. I Cor. 1.22). Its purpose is to highlight the *interpretation* of the feeding that follows it in 8.14–21.

And yet we must also notice that it is a saying about disciple-ship in reverse. As we have seen, 8.22–26, the healing of the blind man points ahead to the central section of Mark's gospel, the three predictions of the passion and their much fuller elaboration of the meaning of discipleship. The threefold pattern of chs. 8, 9 and 10 points inexorably toward the cross. If the healing of the blind man in 8.22–26 is an anticipation of the suffering Son of Man revela-tion, then the feeding of the four thousand, its interpretation *and* the refusal of a sign all combine to reject the simple authority-christology which the Jews seem to expect or even demand. Discipleship is only explicable from the cross. All other attempts,

[13] Cf. Dibelius, *Tradition,* p. 230.

those of the Pharisees and of Peter, are misleading. But progress is being made!

## The Extent and Character of the Q Material

As the previous discussion has shown, there is some evidence to suggest that the saying refusing a sign was part of the pre-Markan tradition and that Mark had not reworked it to any great extent when he inserted it into his gospel. The opposite is the case with the Q tradition as reflected in Matthew and Luke. Here we have a similar saying which has been extensively reworked by the Q community and later adapted by Matthew and Luke as they seek to incorporate it into their Gospels. The evidence for an early tradition about refusing a sign lies primarily in the common form and vocabulary of Mark and Q. Both accounts share the words: sign (σημεῖον), generation (γενεά), shall be given (δοθήσεται). Both accounts also share a specific context, i.e. a concern to deny the Jewish request for the sign as an authenticating proof of the authority of Jesus. This anti-Jewish apologetic purpose is the reason for the inclusion of the saying in both Mark and Q, the fact that the early tradition thought of the request for the sign as a demand for some sort of divine decree. It is this demand which Jesus refuses to fulfil.

The Q community has transmitted a version of the refusal saying with an exception attached: 'no sign, except the sign of Jonah'. If the Markan version is dependent upon an older form of the saying, then either Mark has dropped the exception clause or Q has inserted it. It is the latter alternative which I suggest is the correct one.

Our first task is to explain the extent and character of the Q version of the Sign of Jonah saying (Matt. 12.38–42; Matt. 16.1–4; Luke 11.16, 29–32). A careful study of Matthew and Luke reveals at once that the double saying about the witness of the Ninevites and of the Queen of the South (Luke 11.31f. = Matt. 12.41f.) is almost exactly the same in Matthew and Luke. The order of the saying is reversed by Matthew or Luke, but even so, the agreement is precise enough to extend to the very verb which is used in each comparison: ἀναστήσονται in the Ninevite statement and ἐγερθήσεται in the Queen of the South comparison. The one specific change occurs in Luke 11.31, where a characteristic Lukan phrase 'the men of this generation', rather than the simpler 'this generation', is found. Thus there is good reason to suppose that the double saying was part of the Q tradition and that it was placed after the Sign of Jonah saying in Q.

In the sign-saying itself the reconstruction of Q is complicated by the fact that this incident is reported twice in Matthew, at 12.38–40 and 16.1–4. The report in Matt. 16 is close to Mark in vocabulary *and* it occurs in the same order of events as does Mark 8.11–13. This situation is helpful because we are enabled to see the impact that Mark has had upon Matthew and can be more precise about the influence and extent of the Q version of the incident. The vocabulary that Matt. 16.1–4 shares with Mark 8.11–13 which is *not* found in Q is: testing (πειράζοντες), from heaven (ἐκ τοῦ οὐρανοῦ), a partially similar verb in the introduction (προσελθόντες compared with Mark's ἐξῆλθον) and the same verb at the conclusion (ἀπῆλθεν). Matt. 12 is more of an indication of Q than is Matt. 16; and the use of this information in relation to Luke 11.16, 29–30 helps delineate Q.

As might be expected, very little of the introductory material can be ascribed to Q. Luke has the most obvious variation when he places the request for a sign in 11.16 and then delays the reply till 11.29. The insertion of four units of material between the request and the reply, or, conversely, the insertion of the request in the Beelzebul pericope, would seem to be a clear indication of Luke's editorial and theological tendencies rather than any evidence of Q. Matthew does not have any similar reworking of the introduction. The only thing in common is the word 'sign' (σημεῖον), which is also in Mark's introduction, and the preposition ἐκ (τοῦ οὐρανοῦ) over against Mark's ἀπό. The nature of the introduction in Q remains a mystery. This judgment is confirmed by the similarity of the introductions in Matt. 12 and 16.

The Q version of Jesus' reply is easier to determine. Both Matt. 12.39 and 16.4 and Luke 11.29 agree against Mark in qualifying 'this generation' as evil (πονηρά). These three verses also have identical wording for the refusal itself: καὶ σημεῖον οὐ δοθήσεται αὐτῇ εἰ μὴ τὸ σημεῖον Ἰωνᾶ. Mark has the same verb but is otherwise quite different. Matt. 12.39 adds the explanation 'the prophet' after Ἰωνᾶ at the end of the sentence. Agreement which is as extensive as this

demands that we consider Q to have contained a refusal of a sign
*and* the added reference to the Sign of Jonah.

The real problem, however, is the relation between Luke 11.30
and Matt. 12.40, the explanations of the Sign of Jonah. The vast
difference between Luke and Matthew has apparently caused
scholars to overlook the structural similarity which underlies
these two explanations. If we set out both sentences in outline
form, it becomes clear that we have a structural similarity which
has been filled in with varying content, i.e. it is the eschatological
correlative which was described above.[14]

| Luke 11.30: | Matt. 12.40: |
|---|---|
| καθὼς γὰρ ἐγένετο Ἰωνᾶς τοῖς Νινευείταις σημεῖον, | ὥσπερ γαρ ἦν Ἰωνᾶς ἐν τῇ κοιλίᾳ τοῦ κήτους τρεῖς ἡμέρας καὶ τρεῖς νύκτας, |
| οὕτως ἔσται καὶ ὁ υἱὸς τοῦ ἀνθρώπου τῇ γενεᾷ ταύτῃ. | οὕτως ἔσται ὁ υἱὸς τοῦ ἀνθρώπου ἐν τῇ καρδίᾳ τῆς γῆς τρεῖς ἡμέρας καὶ τρεῖς νύκτας. |

In outline form the eschatological correlative, which is common to
both verses, is:

$$καθὼς \ (ὥσπερ) - ἐγένετο \ (ἦν) - Ἰωνᾶς - . . . ,$$
$$οὕτως - ἔσται - ὁ \ υἱὸς \ τοῦ \ ἀνθρώπου. . . .$$

In other words, the common element is clearly discernible as is the
obvious individuality of Matthew and Luke. That this is a typical
Q formulation, also used elsewhere, has been argued above. We
need only mention here that the explanations offered by Matthew
and Luke are based upon an earlier Q explanation which was
phrased in a typically Q way; Matthew and Luke are using an
earlier *form*.

To summarize the results up to this point: the introduction to
the Q saying is lost; Jesus' reply is a refusal to give a sign to this
evil generation but with an exception appended to the refusal – no
sign, except the Sign of Jonah; this sign is then explained by
using the eschatological correlative to correlate Jonah and the Son
of Man, but the specific details of the intended parallel are not
recoverable; finally, the Q unit closes with the double saying
(order uncertain) again comparing (unfavourably) this generation

[14] See above in ch. II, pp. 47–58.

with both the Ninevites and the Queen of the South: Jesus is greater than either Jonah or Solomon.

## The Origin of the Q Saying

At this point our problem has only begun. If this is the nature of the Q version of the Sign of Jonah, then we must ask how it reached this form. Mark's report reflects an early tradition. Why does Q contain this particular version of the saying? Or more specifically, why is there a reference to a Sign of Jonah rather than a simple refusal?

If we consider the Q unit as a whole (request, refusal, exception, and explanation), the common theme is that of judgment against this generation. The opponents of Jesus ask for a sign and are refused – to a degree – because they have illustrated that they are evil by demanding a sign ἐκ τοῦ οὐρανοῦ. The double saying, which probably existed independently, makes a similar point: two non-Israelites (the Queen of the South and the people of Nineveh) will rise up at the judgment to condemn this generation for their lack of response to Jesus. He is greater than Jonah and greater than Solomon. Thus, the double saying could easily be attached to the saying refusing a sign. They are both concerned with stating the Q community's judgment against its non-Christian contemporaries, who are most likely Jews. The demand for a sign is associated with the Jews in the gospels as well as in the Pauline corpus (I Cor. 1.22). I suggest that the early tradition concerning the Jewish rejection of Jesus has produced two units of tradition: (1) refusal of a sign and (2) double saying. These two units were combined by the Q community on the basis of its anti-Jewish polemic with a strong emphasis on judgment.

It has been shown above that the impending appearance of the Son of Man is a very characteristic concern of the Q community and that this group is preoccupied with the recognition of the earthly Jesus as the one who will come; the future Son of Man sayings have led to the creation of the present Son of Man sayings. This interest in the sayings of Jesus would centre on those sayings which emphasize the impending judgment. The task of the one who is 'Son of Man designate' is naturally to warn or prepare his followers for his return – and judgment. The Q community is thus engaged in preparing for the imminent appearance of the reign of

God which will be initiated by the coming of the Son of Man. Judgment sayings such as we have in the refusal of a sign and in the double saying would be intended to create a sense of urgency and repentance on the part of those who hear, and hence lead them to consider joining the fellowship of the Son of Man.

Once these two units are combined, because of their similar judgmental purpose, the new insight of the Q community about the nature of the one who had created this fellowship would require a re-evaluation of the tradition about his words. Jesus refused to give a sign to the Pharisees, yet the resurrection or assumption[15] of Jesus to the right hand of God as Son of Man is surely a sign to the Q community. The fellowship continued after Jesus' death because he was now the Son of Man. Not only that, the whole issue of resurrection and judgment had been anticipated in the double saying: the Ninevites and the Queen of the South will rise up and condemn this generation. Surely the recognition of Jesus' assumption to the right hand of God, as coming judge, would be a sign to the contemporaries of the Q community. Jesus *did* give a sign – his assumption is a sign because it has led to the christological cognition which is the foundation of the life of the Q community.

If a sign had been given, according to the understanding of the Q community, how could it be stated? The essential element in the Q understanding of Jesus is the continuity and validity of his teaching. The Jesus who taught among them is also the coming judge; his teaching must therefore be repeated because it has been shown to be of the highest significance; it is the coming judge's testimony about how men are to prepare for his coming. The Q community must continue to teach what Jesus taught because it is the message that will guide men to salvation, that will bring them through the judgment. With this orientation, the solution to the understanding of the sign of Jonah was clear. The double saying refers to the 'Sign' of Jonah, i.e. Jonah is extolled as the great and effective preacher (τὸ κήρυγμα ʼΙωνᾶ Luke 11.32 = Matt. 12.41). And not only that, Jonah is the one who is delivered from death; he is the vindicated preacher.

Thus I suggest that the origin of the Sign of Jonah saying, 'no

[15] The word assumption is used as a technical term to express the idea of Jesus' being taken 'on high' to God. It is to be distinguished from exaltation and resurrection.

sign will be given to this evil generation except the sign of Jonah',
lies in the application of the Q community's theological outlook
to the problem of a sign which is refused by Jesus and yet which
Jesus himself is. The impact of Easter and the continuity of the
fellowship which began during Jesus' earthly ministry have
resulted in an elaboration of the judgment theme. Just as Jesus
himself takes on new meaning for the Q community (the christological cognition), so the sayings of Jesus must be understood
anew from the same perspective.

But source and form analysis indicates that there was an
explanation attached to the exception: 'For as Jonah was a sign
. . . , so the Son of Man will be . . .' The exact wording of the
comparison is not recoverable, but it may have been quite like the
Lukan form of the saying: 'For as Jonah was a sign to the Ninevites, so the Son of Man will be to this generation' (Luke 11.30).
That this is really a possibility is suggested by the other eschatological correlatives which both Matthew and Luke have preserved
from the Q tradition. As explained above in chapter II, the
eschatological correlative is a formal way of bringing together the
past, present, and future, by correlating an Old Testament figure,
or a present phenomenon, with the imminent appearance of the
Son of Man. The three correlatives of Luke 17 (Matt. 24) are much
simpler than this correlative in Luke 11.30 and Matt. 12.40. In
Luke 11.30 we have not merely the correlation of the *days* of Jonah
with those of the future Son of Man, but rather the added element
of the *Sign* of Jonah correlated with the Son of Man. It is because
of this more complex elaboration of the eschatological correlative
that one must assume that the form is being used by the Q community to clarify the new insight which had already led them to
say, 'except the sign of Jonah'. In other words, the original use of
the eschatological correlative to give content to the Son of Man
expectation is being modified because it is used here in a different,
though related, context. It is still the context of judgment which
stresses the continuity of the Son of Man with Jesus, but it is also
a statement about the significance of Jesus as the preacher who is
now at the right hand of God. An established form from the Q
community is being adapted to serve a slightly different purpose;
the Q community is itself developing or extending the use of the
eschatological correlative.

We should also note that the expansion of the saying about

refusing a sign into the Sign of Jonah saying is a clarification of the enigmatic conclusion to the Ninevite comparison in the double saying: 'A greater thing than Jonah is here' (Luke 11.32 = Matt. 12.41). The limited greatness of Jonah is his preaching, therefore the absolute greatness of Jesus must be stated.

What is the meaning of the Q version of the saying? The phrase, 'the sign of Jonah', is the result of Q's tendency to correlate Old Testament figures with the Son of Man in the context of judgment. Both σημεῖον and Ἰωνᾶ come from the tradition which Q has received and combined – σημεῖον from the saying about refusing a sign and Ἰωνᾶ from the double saying. The correlation of Jonah and Son of Man was expressed as *the Sign* of Jonah and the Son of Man. The whole phrase became difficult to interpret as a result; but I suggest that the intent of the correlation here is similar to that in the other three eschatological correlatives, namely, that the figure Jonah has meaning primarily because he is a preacher of repentance, prior to a great judgment (as the Q community thought Jesus was also). Secondly, Jonah is also one who has overcome death, as Jesus has. Both are vindicated preachers.

The failure to find any pre-Christian mention of 'the Sign of Jonah' is easily explained: the phrase is created by the Q community in its elaboration of the significance of Jesus. The fortuitous juxtaposition of the saying refusing a sign and the double saying establishes the context from which the phrase 'sign of Jonah' can emerge. Since the eschatological correlative tradition has already established a precedent in the Q community, it is used in this passage to correlate Jonah and the Son of Man. The phrase 'sign of Jonah' is not an item of previous theological discussion but a unique development within the Q community. It is for this reason, then, that the Sign of Jonah can be an important indication of the theological stance of the Q community: the Sign of Jonah is a direct statement of their christology.

To summarize this section: two independent units of judgment tradition have been combined and elaborated by the Q community because of its understanding of Jesus as judge, as the future Son of Man, and as the one who is raised to be seated at God's right hand. They rely on their own formal language to clarify the comparison which they see between Jonah and Jesus. The confusion of later interpreters is partially the result of their having used the eschatological correlative in a new context and with a varied terminology, that is, with the introduction of the word 'sign' in an eschatological correlative comparison.

## The Theological Implications of the Q Community's Redaction

One of the most obvious implications of this analysis is the re-assessment of the future Son of Man sayings. Tödt and others have argued that the future Son of Man sayings are authentic while Vielhauer and Perrin have in different ways attempted to show that the entire Son of Man tradition is a creation of the early church.[16] All would agree that it is in Q that we find the first significant use of the future Son of Man sayings, whether from Jesus or not. Now, however, with the isolation of the eschatological correlative *and* its development within the Q material, as well as its careful reflection of the Q theology, we have additional evidence to argue that the Son of Man tradition does *originate* in the Q community and is based upon the *pesher* interpretation of a very early *Mar* christology.

The Q community was not only interested in the Son of Man as future, but also in the teachings of Jesus as the Son of Man in his earthly ministry. It was interested because it saw the importance of his teaching in the light of its present understanding of him as the coming judge. To follow Jesus' teaching is to be prepared for his coming; to follow and be prepared means to participate in the fellowship which defines one as a disciple. It has long been recognized that the Q material shows a marked interest in the problem of discipleship,[17] and this is borne out in what we have seen in the Sign of Jonah material. The Q community is seeking to inform everyone of the situation which it perceives, and it is a situation of danger to those who do not follow Jesus, or do not become attached to the fellowship which is based upon his warning and teaching. Discipleship is dependent upon a recognition of Jesus as Son of Man designate, as the one who was vindicated by his assumption and whose teaching therefore must be considered crucial. There is no attempt on the part of the Q community to emphasize the death of Jesus. The passion kerygma is not part of the Q concern. Tödt points out that its use of the Old Testament does not even hint at such an understanding; and that

---

[16] See above in ch. II, pp. 48 and 58.
[17] Cf. Tödt, *Son of Man,* pp. 232–46, 306–11.

is certainly the case with the Sign of Jonah. That Jesus died is not a matter of concern; he is now alive and on high and will soon come. Later we shall see that Matthew has combined the passion kerygma of Mark with the Sign of Jonah saying and completely changed the purpose of the saying as first presented by Q.

*Composition Analysis*

Redaction criticism has assumed that the composition of a gospel, or the ordering of the material, can be of assistance in clarifying the theology of the writer. Whether he is merely copying the arrangement of an earlier source or not, the order or structure of the finished piece is a reflection of his own understanding. In an analysis of Q, since we have no certain information about the order, we can only conjecture on the basis of limited clues. We should certainly not be justified in drawing elaborate conclusions about the Q theological stance based upon the apparent original order and extent of Q. However, there does seem to be corroboration of certain factors concerning order if we consider Taylor's analysis along with the present arrangement of Matthew and Luke; i.e. there are certain collections of material which do seem to be the result of the creative activity of the Q community. If this is so, then we are justified in seeking a unified answer to the problem of the theology of Q by an analysis of the context created by any definite aggregate of material.

The Sign of Jonah appears to be part of such a collection of material. Using Luke as our basis, a small collection exists of the following:

| *Luke* | | *Matthew* |
|---|---|---|
| 11.14–23 | Beelzebul accusation | 12.22–30 |
| 11.24–26 | The Return of the Evil Spirit | 12.43–45 |
| 11.29–32 | The Sign of Jonah | 12.38–42 |

The pericope 'the Sin against the Holy Spirit' is placed by Matthew at 12.31–37 under the influence of Mark; the Lukan parallel (12.10) is not related to this group of sayings and shows signs of having an independent existence. It is probably Matthew who has inserted this Q saying into this collection.

What do these three sayings have in common that would lead

the Q community to place them together? The unifying theme is a warning about the response to Jesus. All three stress the fact that judgment will come upon those who do not recognize Jesus as the one who judges, as the coming Son of Man. Those who do respond are those who are prepared for the judgment.

The overriding problem for the Q community is the mission, usually the Jewish mission, which for Q means bringing followers into the fellowship of those who are disciples of Jesus. Those who have not accepted the fellowship have accused Jesus of casting out demons by Beelzebul; they have demanded a sign, even after the sign has been specifically indicated as the resurrection and the preaching; they are like the man who is seven times worse after his 'cure'. These three sayings combine to play on one theme although there are overtones of many other issues.

The Beelzebul accusation and the demand for a sign are two examples of the perversity of 'this generation'. The Q context for the Beelzebul accusation is the actual performance of a healing, of the casting out of a demon. The exorcism is a sign which, though ambiguous, is clearly pointed to by Jesus as a sign of the presence of the work of God; it does not go unexplained. Yet there is no positive response shown to the action of healing.

The inclusion of the saying about the Return of the Evil Spirit in the same context as Beelzebul and Jonah is based upon both the catchword 'spirit' and the implied judgment upon those who do not allow the Spirit of God to replace the evil spirit when it has been expelled.

As a collection from Q, these three sayings are part of that community's efforts to correlate the expectation of the near future with the events of the recent past and of the Old Testament. They all combine to show the missionary interest of those within the fellowship. God's activity in Jesus is available, but at a cost; it is also costly to neglect the love shown to men in Jesus.


LUKE'S USE OF THE SIGN OF JONAH TRADITION

*The Extent of Luke's Redaction*

Luke's report of the Sign of Jonah saying is almost entirely based upon the Q version and is not greatly influenced by the Markan saying refusing a sign. We have assumed that he maintains the Q context of the saying, i.e. placing it close to the Beelzebul accusation and *not* in the pre-Caesarea Philippi report. He does share the Markan interest in the demand for a sign as a testing of Jesus (πειράζοντες in Luke 11.16. cf. Mark 8.11) and he agrees with Mark against Matthew in using a simple form of the verb for seeking (ζητεῖ Luke 11.16 and Mark 8.11; cf. Matt. 12.38 ἐπιζητεῖ). The demand is reported in indirect discourse, as in Mark and Matt. 16, and not in direct discourse, as in Matt. 12.

The Lukan peculiarities are the significant elements. Most obvious is the lack of a specific statement about those who demand a sign; rather than Pharisees (Mark) or scribes and Pharisees (Matt. 12), or Pharisees and Sadducees (Matt. 16), Luke has a vague reference to others (ἕτεροι). Many have suggested that this is likely to be a reflection of the Q report, but it seems more reasonable to assume a probable widening of the meaning of 'this generation' to include others besides a specific sect in Judaism. Luke's interest does move beyond Judaism, as Acts illustrates, and he may be indicating this wider concern for man-in-general by making the demand a part of the activity of the crowd.

In 11.29 the reply of Jesus is described as occurring 'when the crowd was increasing' (τῶν δὲ ὄχλων ἐπαθροιζομένων). It is probable that this is an editorial addition to smooth out the transition from the preceding unit which refers to a smaller group of people. On the other hand, it could be part of Luke's attempt to stress the breadth of the accusation against this generation which follows in the Sign of Jonah saying.

Luke 11.30 is Luke's version of the explanation of the sign: 'For as Jonah was a sign to the Ninevites, so that Son of Man will be to this generation.' We have already identified the form of this sentence as the work of Q and the remainder may be from Luke or from Q. Whether it is from Luke or Q, the fact that it appears this way in Luke is in itself evidence of Luke's theological concern. The material in question is the phrase 'to the Ninevites' and 'to this generation'. As Vögtle pointed out, the real problem arises when the Sign of Jonah is qualified by these datives, especially in the parallel between the Ninevites and this generation.[18] Before this question can be adequately answered, i.e. whether this might be Luke's wording or Q's, we must look carefully at the context in which Luke has placed the entire incident.

[18] Vögtle, 'Jonaszeichen', p. 272.

*Composition Analysis*

Luke's travel section begins at 9.51 where the decision is made to go to Jerusalem. From 9.51 to 13.30 Luke has very little material from Mark and has apparently relied heavily on Q and the special material (the so-called 'L'). There can be little doubt that Luke is composing a type of discipleship discourse throughout this entire section: from 10.1, when the seventy are commissioned, through the Good Samaritan parable (10.29–37), to parables of the Mustard Seed and Leaven (13.18–21), Luke is collecting and editing material which assists in defining the nature of a disciple. It is in the midst of this collection that Luke has placed the Sign of Jonah incident.

Probably the most important and obvious indication of Luke's hand is the separation of the *request* (11.16) for a sign from the *reply* (11.29f.) by Jesus. In 11.16 Luke has inserted the requested immediately after certain 'others' have accused Jesus of being in league with Beelzebul. The problem this raises is obvious when we read in 11.17 that Jesus 'knowing their thoughts, says . . .' Why is it necessary to 'know' their thoughts when they have made themselves quite clear by asking for a sign? Matthew shows no indication that this verse belongs here in Q, even though he is very close to Luke at many other points. Thus, Luke has moved the request for a sign back to the beginning of the Beelzebul accusation apparently to make sure that the relation between the two demands or accusations is not lost. We have already seen that Q had previously combined these two incidents; Luke is simply making it more obvious with an editorial emendation.

Since Luke has made a change in the structure, we must then consider the material between 11.16 and 11.29 to be related and probably arranged by Luke for some purpose. The section from 11.14 to 12.20 contains the following:

| *Luke* | | *Mark* |
|---|---|---|
| 11.14–23 | Beelzebul accusation – with strong man parable. Mark and Q. | 3.22–27 |
| 11.24–26 | Return of the evil spirit. Q. | |
| 11.27f. | Speech about true blessedness. L. | |
| 11.29–32 | Sign of Jonah and double saying. Mark and Q. | (8.11–12) |
| 11.33 | Parable about light. Mark. | 4.21 |

| *Luke* | | *Mark* |
|---|---|---|
| 11.34–36 | Parable about the healthy eye. Q. | |
| 11.37–54 | Against the Pharisees and lawyers. Mark and Q. | 7.1–9 |
| 12.1 | Leaven of the Pharisees. Mark. | 8.14–15 |
| 12.2–9 | Exhortation to fearless confession. Q. | |
| 12.10 | Sin against the Holy Spirit. Mark and Q. | 3.28–30 |
| 12.11f. | Assistance of the Holy Spirit. Mark. | 13.11 |

The climax of this section is in 12.11f., where the Holy Spirit becomes the effective countermeasure to the lack of response which the non-Christians have demonstrated in various ways. It is Luke who has put the Assistance of the Holy Spirit pericope immediately after the Sin against the Holy Spirit saying; they are separated in Mark and Matthew. As a climax for Luke, these two sayings serve to close the discussion about spirits and demons, making clear that, far from being in league with Beelzebul, the whole Christian programme is directed against the evil demons and their prince, that Christians are led by the Holy Spirit and are under his influence. Beginning with the Beelzebul accusation, discipleship is viewed from the perspective of the opposition to Jesus, i.e. those who doubt his authority. By placing the Return of the Evil Spirit immediately after the Beelzebul story, as Matthew does not, Luke describes those who make the accusation. If the Holy Spirit does not replace the influence of the evil spirits who leave or are cast out, the final result is the opposite of what might be expected. Then true blessedness (11.27f.) is defined by a reference to those who do God's will, as the opponents do not when they demand a sign. Doing and seeing are related, as the two light parables (11.33–36) seem to show. This generation is partially defined when Luke inserts the discourse against the Pharisees (11.37–54) and follows it with the statement about the Leaven of the Pharisees (12:1). Rather than hypocrisy, fearless confession is what is demanded by God (12.2–9) and even here the Christian does not stand alone; he is aided by the Holy Spirit (12.10–12).

Luke has inserted certain Q and Markan traditions into a collection which begins and ends with two connected pericopes from Mark: Beelzebul (Mark 3.22–27) stands at the beginning and the Holy Spirit sayings at the end (Sin against the Holy Spirit, Mark 3.28–30; Assistance of the Holy Spirit, Mark 13.11). Since both Mark and Q have a report of the Beelzebul problem, the Q material is also called upon. Within this collection is the Sign of Jonah. Luke does not follow Mark's order, but he does seem to know the Markan version; not only because of his vocabulary but also because of the Leaven of the Pharisees saying in Luke 12.1 which is related to Mark's saying in 8.14f., i.e. right after the refusing a sign saying in 8.11–13.

The remainder of ch. 12 and the beginning of ch. 13 (12.13–13.17) show no dependence on Mark at all and are a combination of Q and L material. Thus we are justified by sources as well as by subject matter in considering the break to occur between 12.12 and 12.13, just as the Beelzebul incident begins a new section after the discourse on prayer (11.1–13).

Within this context, Luke uses the Sign of Jonah to emphasize the character of discipleship – in reverse. Rather than accuse Jesus of being in league with the demons, the disciple recognizes in Jesus' healings the 'finger of God', the word of God as King. 'This generation' is typical of those Jews and others who have never been willing to see the greatness of the men of God, such as Solomon and Jonah. In concert with Luke's major programme, we must recognize the universalist emphasis as the one which he would not have overlooked. The addition of the phrase 'to the Ninevites' would have that effect. The gospel is for all, and the Jews are not the only ones who have rejected Jesus, but rejection is made by men of any nation or race. The distinction to be made is between those who respond and those who do not, as this generation does not. It is a matter of disciple versus non-disciple; those who respond to the message of Jesus and those who do not. The True Blessedness saying (11.27f.) which precedes the Sign of Jonah helps to emphasize just this point, as do the two following parables about light and the eye (11.33–36). 'Seeing' and 'doing' go hand in hand for Luke; those who recognize Jesus become those who follow Jesus. Repentance and forgiveness, as major Lukan themes, seem to be very much a part of the background of this arrangement of the material.

*Luke as the Heir of Q*

The general understanding of Luke which is offered by
Conzelmann and others has pointed to Luke's historical interest
along with his development of a theology of the emerging church.
The historicizing of Mark's kerygma and the impact of the new
life under the Spirit have created a situation in which Luke must
redefine the nature of discipleship. It is for this reason that we find
a great deal of Q teaching material in Luke. The Q community is
not interested in the extended eschatology of Luke, but by its concern for the teaching of Jesus and the continuity of that teaching
in the situation after Easter, it has provided Luke with material
which he can use to describe the *life* of Jesus. Since Q continues to
teach the imminence of the kingdom of God and to warn those
who now stand at the threshold of a new age, it can supply the
basic material which Luke now uses for a more historical purpose,
to tell what it was that was taught by Jesus. But for Luke, the
disciple must now readjust to that teaching and carry it over into
the new age of the Spirit where it can take on a more extended
moral emphasis. The judgment is real, though distant, for Luke.
With a slight shift in orientation, much of the Q material can
become part of the Lukan presentation.

The most striking point of continuity between Luke and Q lies
in the understanding of the nature of redemption. As stated in
chapter II, Luke has been careful to avoid the passion kerygma
interpretation which Mark has proposed.[19] As Conzelmann points
out, it is in the book of Acts that this characteristic of Luke's
theology is most clearly presented. Redemption is based upon the
repentance and forgiveness which God offers to all men, it is
founded on the new life which has been made available through
the resurrection of his Son.[20] As is the case with Q, the purpose of
Jesus is to warn about the end (near or far) and to create the new
fellowship of those who have recognized Jesus as the coming Son
of Man. It is the resurrection which is the foundation of this
assurance – and especially the results of Jesus' resurrection, the
ascension and the subsequent sending of the Spirit. The nature of
the fellowship of the Q community is now made more explicit in
Luke with the tradition about Pentecost. The Spirit becomes a

[19] Cf. his rejection of Mark 10.45b.
[20] Conzelmann, *Luke*, p. 201.

specific symbol for the fact of the fellowship and ties it more precisely to the resurrection of Jesus. It was necessary that Jesus die; but redemption does not come through his suffering, it comes in his resurrection and subsequent exaltation.

Luke's highly developed *kyrios* christology has its beginnings in the *Mar* christology of the Q community. In Q the shift toward the recognition of the authority of the earthly Jesus is beginning and is developed in one direction by Mark and in a different direction by Luke. The Lord is exalted at God's right hand, he will come again as judge, and he sends the spirit to aid those who wish to prepare for his coming. Thus, the Lord's earthly sayings have a significance which is historical as well as existential.

When Luke uses the Old Testament, it is used historically – and that is the case with Jonah. Jonah is the great preacher of repentance who as such was a 'sign' to the Ninevites. 'This generation' must mean, for Luke, the generation which is contemporary with Jesus as well as those who are the readers of his gospel. Whether Luke added the two datives in 11.30 or not, they illustrate that Luke finds meaning in the person of Jonah because of his preaching of repentance and undoubtedly because he is successful, that is, vindicated by God. The future verb in 11.30b does not create any problem for Luke because he is reporting a statement of a past era, the mid-point of time, which is, in its historical context, a reference to the future. The Son of Man is one who, from the immediate context of 11.30, will continue to preach and be vindicated by God, even though from the reader's point of view, it is a matter of past event. Thus Luke would have little trouble taking over the old tradition of the eschatological correlative and perhaps adding the datives to make it more precise.

In many ways then, the use of this pericope by Luke shows his affinities with the Q community. The situation for Matthew, to which we now turn, is quite different.

## MATTHEW'S USE OF THE SIGN OF JONAH TRADITION

### The Distinctiveness of Matthew's Reformulation

Part of the uniqueness of Matthew's version of the Sign of Jonah lies in the double report of the incident in Matt. 12.38–42 and 16.1–4, and partly in the direct quotation of Jonah 2.1 in Matt. 12.40. Both of these issues will be taken up in the following sections. Our concern for the present is to describe Matthew's accounts and their place in the history of the tradition.

Matthew's two accounts show that he had had available to him the Q material as well as the Markan report and that he uses each one in its own context. Following the Markan outline, Matthew has placed the Q version close to the Beelzebul accusation, where he found it in Q, and the Markan version he parallels with Mark 8.11–13. As was indicated above, the vocabulary of 12.38–42 is close to Luke and the vocabulary of 16.1–4 is closer to Mark. We must now examine the specific Matthean redaction.

Matthew follows Mark in the explicit citation of those who demand a sign: Mark calls them Pharisees while Matthew calls them scribes and Pharisees in 12.38 and Pharisees and Sadducees in 16.1. Matthew also uses the word πειράζοντες to describe the demand for a sign in ch. 16 and *not* in ch. 12; both Mark and Luke use πειράζοντες. Again, Matt. 16 agrees with Mark and Luke and against Matt. 12 in describing the demanded sign as a sign 'from heaven' (Mark: ἀπό; Matthew 16 and Luke: ἐκ). It is quite clear that Matt. 12 has been less influenced by Mark and is more a reflection of Q and Matthew's own theology. In 12.38 Jesus is directly addressed as διδάσκαλε and the request for a sign is written in direct discourse, not the indirect report of Mark, Matt. 16 and Luke.

The reply of Jesus is almost identical in Matt. 12 and 16 except for the addition in 16.2b–3 of a saying about the signs of the times and signs of the sky. Matt. 12.39 adds the qualification τοῦ προφήτου to the name Ἰωνᾶ. The account in ch. 16 then ends with the remark: 'So he left them and departed' (cf. Mark 8.13). In ch. 12, however, the Sign of Jonah is explained (12.40) and the double saying is appended.

There can be no doubt that the tradition reaches its most complex and developed form here in Matthew. The two accounts of the request and the similarities and differences all point to a well worked out solution. We now turn to the two basic problems which this material offers – the quotation from Jonah 2.1 and the existence of the doublet, and their related problems.

*The Significance of the Quotation in Matthew 12.40*

Matthew represents the latest stage in the development of the Sign of Jonah. He has taken over from Q the double saying, though it seems likely that he has reversed it in order to put the Ninevite reference immediately after his quotation, a change which would allow some of the original judgment implications to be added to the descent interpretation which Matthew imposes.

It is the quotation from the Septuagint of Jonah 2.1, which Matthew inserts in the eschatological correlative to clarify his understanding of the reference to Jonah, which gives us the clearest indication of his purpose. The quotation is exactly that of the text of the Septuagint, which is at this point an exact rendering of the Massoretic text. Stendahl has suggested that the quotation was added after the book was completed, since a direct quotation without a typical introduction does not fit Matthew's normal pattern.[21] This seems somewhat far-fetched. Matthew is not working on his own in developing an exegesis or *pesher*, but is replacing the content of the eschatological correlative which he received from Q with a quotation which will clarify the meaning of the refusal and its exception. We have noted that he appears to have this same freedom in the correlatives in ch. 24 where he uses a favourite expression: the parousia of the Son of Man.

Stendahl's suggestion is based on Justin Martyr, *Dialogue with Trypho*, 107.1, where Matt. 12.39 is alluded to and where the interpretation which is stated in Matt. 12.40 is presented by Justin, but with no indication that Justin knows of Matt. 12.40. Surely, Stendahl says, Justin would have used Matt. 12.40 to support his interpretation if it had existed in his text of the gospel.[22] But Strecker comments that there are other problems involved which make the solution more problematical. There is evidence in *Dialogue* 107.2 of text mixing as well as the fact that Justin has confused 12.38 and 16.1. Besides, is Justin referring to the gospel, or is he relying on a post- or pre-Matthean text? Strecker argues that it is best to assume that 12.40 is the work of the evangelist,[23] a decision with which we agree.

The point of the comparison in Matt. 12.40 is the similar *time* spent in the belly of the fish and the heart of the earth. Rabbinic speculation about Jonah's sojourn in the belly of the fish, as well as the implications of the psalm in Jonah 2.2–9, illustrate that the

[21] Stendahl, *Matthew*, pp. 132f.
[22] *Ibid.*
[23] Strecker, *Gerechtigkeit*, pp. 103f.

swallowing was thought to be a journey to the gates of *Sheol*, an experience of death, or at least near-death.[24] The Son of Man will also spend three days and three nights in death. But, of course, the three days and nights also signify that there will be an end to the 'death' and that the Son of Man will return to life just as Jonah returned. The Sign of Jonah, then is his *return to life* after a short time in death. Matthew has chosen to concentrate on the fish incident in the Jonah saga and not on the Ninevite experience.

If Matthew has inserted the Jonah 2.1 quotation into the Q explanation, is there any evidence to suggest the reason for such an inclusion? There are two factors which are peculiar to Matthew which may indicate his thinking: the addition of the word 'prophet' in 12.39 and the specific reference to scribes and Pharisees in 12.38 (cf. 16.1, Pharisees and Sadducees).

Matthew shows interest elsewhere in stating the relation of the fate of Jesus to the fate of the prophets. He often indicts the Jews as those who have killed the prophets.[25] The office of the prophet is one of suffering because of the obstinacy of the Jews in refusing as God's word any word which threatens their world. The mention of the fact that Jonah was a prophet in that pericope where Matthew stresses the suffering of Jonah and Jesus, and not in ch. 16, would point to the passion of Jesus as the significant element in the Jonah comparison. Both Jonah and Jesus suffer for the good of God's work, on behalf of Israel and for the Gentiles. Judgment upon this generation is still evident, but now it is focused to relate to the specific fact of the passion of Christ. It is also of importance that in 12.38 Matthew uses typically prophetic language in accusing this generation: μοιχαλίς is not used by Mark or Luke at this point, though it is found in Mark at 8.38. Perhaps it is related to the suffering Son of Man tradition.

The second indication of Matthew's theological interest is the specific mention of the Pharisees and scribes (12.38) and the Pharisees and Sadducees (16.1). Matthew is preparing for the extensive indictment in ch. 23. His obvious concern to place the burden of opposition upon the 'learned' sects of Judaism leads him to insert these specific references about Jesus' opposition. In Matthew Jesus is primarily the great teacher, the interpreter of

[24] Cf. Jeremias, "Ἰωνᾶς", p. 412. See also: Louis Ginsberg, *The Legends of the Jews* (1938).
[25] Matt. 5.12; 23.30, 31, 37.

the law. His attack is against the misunderstanding of the heritage of Israel, not against the law itself. But the teacher is effective and to be heard because he is the one who died and rose. In a small way, the passion kerygma is combined with the 'authoritative teacher' message in this pericope, and Matthew is revealed as a theologian who has combined both strands of theological tradition into a single unified understanding of Jesus.

Probably the most crucial factor in the quotation is the number 'three'. Here is the real point of Matthew's comparison: both are in death or *Sheol* for three days and three nights. It is this parallel which causes Matthew to quote Jonah 2.1, or at least to quote that section which he does. If his point were that both Jonah and Jesus were dead, why stress the three days and why repeat it in the statement about Jesus? It was only when the three-day tradition had become an integral part of the passion tradition that such a quotation could have been chosen.[26] Matthew, who already recognizes the parallel between Jonah and Jesus to be that of suffering (descent), finds in the text of Jonah an exact correspondence between the lengths of the sojourns of each in *Sheol*. It is the absolute use of three days and three nights which points inexorably toward Matthew's fully developed passion-kerygmatic understanding of the Sign of Jonah and illustrates his incorporation of the Q theology into the passion kerygma.

Whatever the possible origin of the 'three days' or 'on the third day' tradition, by the time we reach Matthew it has become an integral part of the passion kerygma. All three synoptics have reported the triple denial of Jesus by Peter. In Matthew in seven other places 'three' or 'third' is used in a variety of ways, many of them implying an indefinite figure – similar to the English idiom 'a couple of days'. Four times 'three' is used to refer to the time between the death and resurrection; twice it is used with reference to the building up of the temple in three days.

It seems clear, first of all, that there was a close connection made in the early church between the statement about the building up of the temple and the resurrection. It is this statement which Mark uses in the passion account as the prime evidence for the charge of blasphemy. It is referred to in Mark and Matthew as part of the mocking of Jesus while he hangs on the cross: 'You who would destroy the temple and build it in three days, save

[26] Tödt, *Son of Man*, p. 213.

yourself!' (Matt. 27.40). Matthew and Mark have used the three-day tradition more than Luke.

The connection between Jesus and the temple, based on the three days, becomes even more important for Matthew, when we discover that he has also stated: 'a greater thing than the temple is here' (Matt. 12.6). This is the same phrase (except for a different form of the adjective) that we find at the conclusion of the double saying: 'a greater thing than Jonah (or Solomon) is here' (Matt. 12.41f.). What we see in Matthew is a configuration of images surrounding the passion and resurrection story. The three-day imagery has taken on a kind of inclusive meaning which becomes a stable factor in the passion tradition.

Thus it is accurate to suggest that Matthew's particular quotation does point to his heavily passion-oriented understanding of the Sign of Jonah and of the significance of Jesus. He is preparing for the passion predictions of Matt. 16.13ff. (cf. Mark 8.27ff.) by viewing the Son of Man in 12.40 as the *suffering* Son of Man. The creativity of Mark is now working its way back into the Q material: the future Son of Man is at the same time the suffering Son of Man in the mind of Matthew.

### Composition Analysis

It is far beyond our purpose to attempt a complete compositional or structural analysis of Matthew, but analysing the context in which Matthew places the Sign of Jonah may help to indicate more fully what he finds of value in this pericope.

Matthew uses the Sign of Jonah saying twice: 12.40 and 16.4. What is the purpose of the doublet in Matthew's gospel? In a preliminary way, it is clear that 16.1–4 is placed where it is because at this point Matthew is following the order of Mark. Mark 8.11–13 does not contain a mention of the Sign of Jonah but, as shown above, Matt. 16.1–4 is closer to the language and form of Mark than is Matt. 12.38–40. Matt. 12 clearly shows the characteristics typical of Q, primarily the double saying in 12.41f. and the presence of the eschatological correlative in 12.40.

It is likely that the position of 12.38–42 is the result of the influence of Q. Both Matthew and Luke place the Sign of Jonah in close connection with the Beelzebul accusation; Matthew is probably influenced by the outline of Q in his placing of the saying.

12.38–42 is part of the transition section (11.1–12.50) between two of Matthew's major collections of sayings. Chapter 10, the speech on discipleship, is apparently ended at 11.1 when the journey is continued. And yet, the theme of discipleship is obviously carried on throughout chs. 11 and 12. Matthew is developing material on discipleship which, though not direct teaching to the disciples, is yet illustrative of the meaning of discipleship. The climax comes in 12.46–50 where Jesus sums up the whole matter of discipleship with the saying: 'For whoever does the will of my Father who is in Heaven, this one is my brother and sister and mother' (12.50).

It is within this developed elaboration on discipleship that Matthew places the material from Q on Beelzebul, Jonah and the Return of the Evil Spirit. The Sin against the Holy Spirit is inserted after the Beelzebul saying and prior to the Sign of Jonah; here Matthew is following Mark.

We have already noted that Matthew's emphasis in the Sign of Jonah is on the passion kerygma, which seems to dominate Matthew's assessment of that passage. There are peculiar Matthean elements in the other speeches as well. Why this peculiar conflation of Mark and Q?

| Matthew | | Mark | Luke |
|---|---|---|---|
| 12.22–30 | Beelzebul | 3.22–27 | 11.14f., 17–23 |
| 12.31–37 | Sin against the Holy Spirit | 3.28–30 | 12.10; 6.43–45 |
| 12.38–42 | Sign of Jonah | (8.11–13) | 11.16, 29–32 |
| 12.43–45 | Return of the Evil Spirit | | 11.24–26 |
| 12.46–50 | Jesus' True Relatives | 3.31–35 | 8.19–21 |

Matthew has included in the Beelzebul introduction a reference to the Son of David; the response of the crowd (ὄχλοι) to the healing of the blind man is in the form of a question: 'Is not this the Son of David?' Immediately thereafter, the Pharisees accuse Jesus of being in collusion with the Prince of Demons. This confrontation establishes a pattern for the entire section: the Pharisees indicate their unwillingness to be open to the possibility of revelation in Jesus' deeds and thus become a type of the anti-disciple. Matthew has a tendency to use the Son of David title in connection with healings, but it is difficult to see what purpose is served in using it here; it is not picked up in the following material. Perhaps discipleship is partly a willingness to accept miracles as manifestations of Jesus' authority as the Son of David.

Matthew follows Mark in placing the Sin against the Holy Spirit saying (12.31–37) immediately after the Beelzebul pericope. The intent is obvious: to accuse Jesus of being in league with Beelzebul is blasphemy. Matthew has modified Mark in rejecting the words τοῖς υἱοῖς in Mark 3.28 and reports merely that sins and blasphemies will be forgiven men (not Mark's 'sons of men'). But blasphemy against the Spirit will not be forgiven. Then Matthew reports the Q saying which distinguishes between 'speaking against the Son of Man' and 'speaking against the Holy Spirit'.

Matthew closes this section with Q material which Luke has placed elsewhere – about the productivity of a good tree, and the good that comes forth from the good man; 'by your words you will be justified, and by your words you will be condemned' (12.37). There are certain vague resemblances in this material to Q, but the conclusion especially is typically Matthean.

Thus Matthew continues to develop his statement on discipleship in 12.31–37. Blasphemy has been uttered against Jesus by the Pharisees and Matthew agrees with Q that it is possible to forgive those who do not yet understand the significance of Jesus, i.e. before the passion and the resurrection. But it is not clear that the kingdom of God is 'among' this generation, that the Spirit is at work in the life of the church, and therefore that continued rejection of Jesus is the work of the evil 'tree'. It would seem that the generality of the saying about the good tree and the good fruit, etc., is now being specifically applied to this situation. The Beelzebul accusation must have been a serious one in the early church and it has risen to the place of honour as a prime example of the anti-disciple. It ties together the healings of Jesus with the teaching – but is used by Matthew to make sense of what it means to be a disciple. As Matthew moves now toward his conclusion about the true relatives of Jesus, he adds two elements which have come to him from Q, which will help to emphasize the discipleship that he perceives as the correct one.

The refusal to give a sign is found in Mark but not in this context and not with the completeness of the Q version. The language and content give every indication that in 12.38–42 Matthew is following the Q report. The Sign of Jonah is placed here by Q, as we have suggested above, because of the way it illustrates the character of this generation; it serves as a warning. Matthew seems to find this same factor relevant but has apparently made this generation more explicit by reporting that the Pharisees and scribes ask for a sign; and Jesus is addressed as teacher. Thus the antitype continues: those who are not disciples ask for a sign; and the true disciple sees the sign and especially the passion and resurrection as the truly crucial sign which is given; to them Jesus is more than a 'teacher'.

The Return of the Evil Spirit saying follows the Sign of Jonah. Matthew makes clear his understanding of it by appending a final comment: 'Thus it will be for this evil generation.' That is, the last state of the man, which is worse than the first, is the state of those who refuse to allow the Holy Spirit to become part of them and therefore allow the evil spirit, and his friends, to return and to create even more disruption in their lives.[27] The disciple is one who lives with the Holy Spirit and thus can see the signs, the meaning of the healings, etc.

Returning now to Mark, Matthew concludes this long section on discipleship with a fairly close copy of Mark's report of the statement about Jesus' true relatives. The house of Jesus, the true church, is composed of those who see and do the will of God. The disciples are the sons of God, are part of God's family. This is undoubtedly a fitting ending to a discourse on discipleship. Matthew has found a use for both Mark and Q, and in the one major change in the whole last section of ch. 12, the quotation from Jonah 2.1, he has stressed the significance of the passion and death of Jesus, thus pointing ahead to the centrality of that material. The teaching about discipleship is only meaningful when one sees it in the light of the one who is followed, the one who dies and rises – the suffering Son of Man, the judge who first suffers only to rise again.

In ch. 16 Matthew again records a demand for a sign, this time with wording quite close to Mark 8.11f. and in the same order as Mark. However, there are two interesting variations. Those who request the sign are now Pharisees and Sadducees, not just the scribes and Pharisees of ch. 12. And a Q-type proverbial statement

[27] Strecker, *Gerechtigkeit,* pp. 105f.

about the signs of the heavens is inserted before the condemnation of this generation.

16.2b–3

ὀψίας γενομένης λέγετε·
εὐδία, πυρράζει γὰρ ὁ οὐρανός.
καὶ πρωΐ· σήμερον χειμών, πυρράζει γὰρ στυγνάζων ὁ οὐρανός.
τὸ μὲν πρόσωπον τοῦ οὐρανοῦ γινώσκετε διακρίνειν,
τὰ δὲ σημεῖα τῶν καιρῶν οὐ δύνασθε;

There is serious doubt in the minds of some text critics whether this central section of the pericope was originally a part of the work of Matthew.[28] Westcott and Hort decide that 16.2b–3 must be declared secondary: 'Both documentary evidence and the impossibility of accounting for omission prove these words to be no part of the text of Matthew. They can hardly have been an altered repetition of Luke 12.54–56, but were apparently derived from an extraneous source, written or oral, and inserted in the Western text at a very early time.'[29] We must agree that Luke 12.54–56, although showing some similarity, does not appear to be the origin of 16.2b–3:

Luke 12.54–56

ἔλεγεν δὲ καὶ τοῖς ὄχλοις·
ὅταν ἴδητε νεφέλην ἀνατέλλουσαν ἐπὶ δυσμῶν,
εὐθέως λέγετε ὅτι ὄμβρος ἔρχεται, καὶ γίνεται οὕτως.
καὶ ὅταν νότον πνέοντα,
λέγετε ὅτι καύσων ἔσται, καὶ γίνεται.
ὑποκριταί, τὸ πρόσωπον τῆς γῆς καὶ τοῦ οὐρανοῦ οἴδατε δοκιμάζειν,
τὸν καιρὸν δὲ τοῦτον πῶς οὐ δοκιμάζετε;

Both sound very much like proverbial sayings and could have come into the Christian tradition from outside sources.[30] But because the manuscript evidence is not decisive one way or the other, it is not possible to come to a final decision about the text.

However, the problem is not a crucial one. Whether 16.2b–3 is

[28] American Bible Society, *The Greek New Testament,* ed. by Kurt Aland, Matthew Black, Bruce Metzger, and Alan Wikgren (New York: American Bible Society, 1966), and other Greek texts.
[29] Brooke Foss Westcott and Fenton John Hort, *The New Testament in the Original Greek,* Vol. II: Introduction and Appendix (1882), p. 13 of the Appendix.
[30] Bultmann, *History,* p. 126.

finally judged to be authentically Matthean or not, does not modify the function or meaning of the entire passage. It is interesting to note that if we consider 16.2b–3 a part of the text, it does help to explain the meaning of the phrase '[they sought] σημεῖον ἐκ τοῦ οὐρανοῦ' (16.1). The signs of the *face of the heavens* – the redness of the sky in the evening portends fair weather, while redness in the morning portends storminess – are explained. The signs of the *times* are those events not seen by this evil generation, a reference to the miracles and other signs of the activity of God in the work of Jesus. Matthew, following Mark, has prepared for this saying with the accounts of the feeding of the five thousand and of the four thousand, numerous healings, and the walking on the water. Immediately *following* is the saying about the Leaven of the Pharisees with a direct appeal to the feeding miracles. These are the signs of the times.

Matthew is preparing for the great confession of the Christ at Caesarea Philippi and the radical reinterpretation of the nature of the Messiah – the one who suffers. Matthew has repeated the Sign of Jonah 'exception' but has not added any kind of explanation, unless 16.2b–3 is included, probably because one is not needed at this point. The saying has already been explained as an integral part of the passion tradition and the stage is set for the announcement in which Peter's confession is ascribed to God's intervention and not to any natural ingenuity on the part of Peter (16.17). It is only when the full implications of the suffering and rising of the Christ are made known that true sight will result in an understanding of the signs of the times and not just in the signs of the face of the heavens.

Thus in a secondary sense, discipleship is still the theme as the pattern established by Mark unfolds. Matthew has been more explicit in his condemnation of the Pharisees and in the way in which the Sign of Jonah refers to his passion. The teaching is validated by the suffering and resurrection and not only by the resurrection. Matthew represents the full expression of passion apologetic.

## SUMMARY

At the conclusion of chapter I it was suggested that a comprehensive solution to the Sign of Jonah pericopes was possible if redaction criticism were used as a supplement to form criticism.

That goal has been achieved. The history of the tradition outlined in this chapter confirms the original suggestion that the sign of Jonah complex of material is the end result of a conscious modification of the tradition. Each level of the tradition has played a part in creating the very confusing state of the text, although it is the Q community which has offered the most far-reaching modification and therefore is the key to a reconstruction of the history. The history can be summarized as follows.

Mark bears witness to an early saying refusing a sign which also lies behind the Q material. The Semitic quality of the Markan report indicates that the refusal of a sign comes from an early Palestinian environment. Mark has made use of the tradition by placing it in the midst of a more complex collection of material about the rejection of Jesus by the Jews. He has not rewritten the pericope to any great extent.

The Q community, however, has rewritten the incident of the refusal of a sign so that it might be used to express its understanding of the significance of Jesus' resurrection as well as to pronounce a warning upon this generation, especially the Jews. By combining the words 'sign' and 'Jonah', and by placing the exception clause and the explanation between the refusal of the sign and the double saying, the Q community has created a statement affirming a sign. The eschatological correlative form is adapted by the community to express the immense significance of the resurrection of Jesus upon the life of the community as well as upon the lives of those who have not responded to the renewed preaching of the message of Jesus. Thus Q has amplified the refusal of a sign into a major statement of its disciple-oriented christology, quite in contrast to the role it plays in Mark. The future Son of Man is the same as the earthly Jesus; therefore, the past is of crucial significance for the future. The coming judge has been vindicated and will effect a judgment which is continuous with his teaching while on earth.

When Luke receives the tradition from both Mark and Q, he combines the two but places most weight upon the Q report. His phrasing of the eschatological correlative has the effect of placing all the emphasis of the Jonah comparison upon the earthly activity of the Son of Man, even though the future verb is retained. Thus Luke indicates that he is more impressed with the non-passion preparation theology of Q than he is with Mark's passion christology. The close correlation of this saying and the Beelzebul accusation would also point to the significant influence which Q has made upon Luke.

Matthew's redaction is much more extensive and startling. Not only does he report two Sign of Jonah sayings, one from Mark and one from Q, he also adds a quotation from Jonah 2.1 to create a suffering Son of Man saying. The eschatological correlative is decisively modified, illustrating Matthew's freedom and creative ability. The Sign of Jonah is a sign of the suffering and descent of the Son of Man; his redemptive death is prefigured by the fish incident in the Jonah saga. Because the comparison turns on the corresponding time element – the three days and three nights – Matthew indicates that the full-fledged resurrection tradition is the background to his redaction: Jesus rises three days after his death.

Each level of the tradition responded in a different way to the material which it received. It is the assumption of the free creativity with received material which has allowed us to suggest this history of the origin and development of the Sign of Jonah. And the reverse suggestion is then also true: the specific elements of any one report can be used, along with other similar material, to increase our understanding of the theology of that level of the tradition.

# IV

## CONCLUSION

ALTHOUGH THIS study was originally limited to the problem of the Sign of Jonah, it has led to the larger issue of the theology of the Q community and the relation of this theology to other theological traditions in the New Testament. The Sign of Jonah is just one aspect of the multi-faceted problem of the origins of New Testament thought. Some possible lines of inquiry have already been suggested in the body of the thesis – along with some tentative steps toward their solution. It remains for us to set forth some of the wider implications of this study.

From the point of view of method, the application of redaction criticism as a supplement to form criticism is certainly a significant development within the bounds of the broader form-critical programme. Although a redactional study of the gospels had been anticipated by form critics, it has never been expanded into a self-conscious, controlled, systematic method. It was only with the achievement of an accurate and extensive application of form criticism that the stage was set for any further consideration of method. Once form criticism fully understood its task to be the investigation of the response of the early church to the event of Jesus, and not the continuation of a programme to write a life of Jesus, the focus of attention could move to the neglected results of form criticism. This was the identification of the framework into which the author placed the small traditional units, or the larger preliminary collections of units. Rather than rely on a type of motif criticism to understand the thought of the redactor, it is now possible to examine carefully the small yet significant changes being made in the tradition handed down from the past. In other words, the raw material for a study of the theology of the evangelist is vastly increased. A less static and more open redaction, within certain controlled limits, is now becoming more and more apparent.

Because redaction criticism is still in the early stages of growth, there must be continued reflection upon the method itself as well as upon its results. The distinction between redaction and composition analysis made in this thesis, although not a new one, is upheld by this work and even demanded by the Q material. The difficulty of examining a document whose final form is unknown, requires that more weight be put upon the hints of redaction, just as the opposite is the case with Mark. The method must be flexible enough to adjust to the significant differences in editorial technique used by each redactor. The primary question is: What evidence can be uncovered which would show us the work of the editor upon the material handed down to him? Structure is certainly one clue but, in the case of Q, it is a very limited factor and must be restricted to the small collections of individual units.

Secondly, the results of the application of this method point to a freely creative use of older traditions by the early communities as well as by the evangelists proper. The continuity with the early church would seem to be a continuity of understanding and not a continuity of written texts and documents. The prime interest of these early groups is proclamation and its accompanying elaboration of their faith. For the Q community, at least, the recollection of the past is of secondary importance. Although proclamation and recollection are not mutually exclusive activities, they are distinct. The discovery of the priority of one or the other will assist in unravelling the theological character of those who are responsible for the Q material. The fact that the proclamation takes the form of warning and exhortation, is further evidence for discounting the importance of recollection. The preservation of the past is simply a minor part in preparation for the future, a preparation which is accomplished by a stress upon the crucial character of the present. In this environment, free creativity is merely an aspect of the proclamation. When we move beyond Q to Mark, the same general tendency is found. Both Matthew and Luke have become more than proclaimers, approaching the level of historians where the reporting of past events is a more central concern than it had been for Q and Mark. We would expect Q to be freer with tradition and that Mark would be only slightly less creative – and the evidence in this study substantiates that inference.

From a still wider perspective, the results of this study suggest that the continued use of redaction criticism may eventually lead to a full clarification of the multiple origins of New Testament theology. The possibility of an original diversity of theological traditions, all dependent upon a variety of understandings of Jesus and his significance, rather than an original overarching unity, seems to account for the synoptic evidence with more precision. In contrast to the common opinion of a gradual differentiation of an original 'orthodoxy', the later New Testament situation should now be seen as a continuance of different traditions and not as the development of a series of splinter theologies. The non-passion tradition of Q and Luke is significantly different from Paul, Mark and Matthew to warrant further investigation for a substantiation of the early and primitive nature of this preparation theology. It is now clear that Q is not just the result of a documentary hypothesis but represents a legitimate, independent, theological point of view. The investigation of the titles of Jesus, such as Son of Man and Son of God, has been the crucial starting point and will continue to be important in the future.

Finally, the role of the Old Testament (and related Jewish materials) in the theological traditions of the early communities must be completely reassessed. There is every indication that the Old Testament has been a much more creative factor in determining the shape and content of the Christian traditions. Because of the radically new orientation of the Christian communities – a stance which demands expression – the Old Testament and other Jewish traditions are searched as a possible source of images or concepts which can supply the church with content for its new stance. Thus there are three elements which are interrelated in a complex way: (1) the new understanding of the present, (2) the material of the past, such as the Old Testament, and (3) the recollection of the immediate past, especially the ministry of Jesus. Instead of stressing the third factor, the recollection of the ministry of Jesus, as many source critics do, to the detriment of the other two elements, we must emphasize the first item, the new understanding of the present, as the dominant concern of the early communities. The second and third items, then, are significant because they are integrated with, and used as sources for, the expression of the new understanding.

The study of the Sign of Jonah saying has thus led to new insight into the community, Q, which produced it and to a new recognition of the intricate interrelation of recollection, Old Testament and self-understanding.

# SELECTED BIBLIOGRAPHY

Words printed in bold type are the short titles used in footnotes.

Aland, Kurt (ed.), *Synopsis Quattuor Evangeliorum,* 2nd ed., Stuttgart: Württembergische Bibelanstalt, 1964.

Allen, Willoughby C., *The Gospel According to St Matthew* (International Critical Commentary) Edinburgh: T. & T. Clark, and New York: Charles Scribner's Sons, 1907.

American Bible Society, *The Greek New Testament,* ed. K. Aland, M. Black, B. Metzger, and A. Wikgren, New York: American Bible Society, 1966.

Bacon, Benjamin Wisner, *Studies in Matthew,* London: Constable, and New York: H. Holt and Co., 1930.

Beardslee, William A., *Literary Criticism of the New Testament,* Guides to Biblical Scholarship, Philadelphia: Fortress Press, 1970.

— 'The Wisdom Tradition and the Synoptic Gospels', *JAAR* XXXV (1967), 231–40.

Beare, Francis Wright, *The Earliest Records of Jesus,* Oxford: Basil Blackwell, and Nashville, Tenn.: Abingdon Press, 1962.

Best, Ernest, *The **Temptation** and the Passion: The Markan Soteriology* (Society for New Testament Studies Monograph No. 2), Cambridge: Cambridge University Press, 1965.

Black, Matthew, *An Aramaic Approach to the Gospels and Acts,* 3rd ed., Oxford: Clarendon Press, 1967.

Blass, Fredrich Wilhelm, and Debrunner, A., *A Greek Grammar of the New Testament and other Early Christian Literature,* translation and revision of 9th–10th German edition by Robert W. Funk, Chicago: University of Chicago Press, and Cambridge: Cambridge University Press, 1961.

Bonner, Campbell, 'Traces of Thaumaturgic Technique in the Miracles', *HTR* XX (1927), 171–81.

Bonsirven, Joseph, S. J., *The Theology of the New Testament,* trans.

S. F. L. Tye, London: Burns and Oates, and Westminster, Md.: Newman Press, 1963.

Bornkamm, Günther, *Jesus of Nazareth,* trans. Irene and Fraser McLuskey with James M. Robinson, London: Hodder and Stoughton, and New York: Harper and Row, 1960.

Bornkamm, Günther, Barth, Gerhard, and Held, Heinz Joachim, *Tradition and Interpretation in* **Matthew,** trans. Percy Scott (NTL), 1963.

Borsch, Frederick Houk, *The Son of Man in Myth and History* (NTL), 1967.

Bousset, Wilhelm, *Kyrios Christos* (FRLANT 21), 3rd ed., 1926.

Brown, J. P., 'Mark as Witness to an Edited Form of Q', *JBL* LXXX (1961), 29–44.

Bultmann, Rudolf, **History** *of the Synoptic Tradition,* trans. John Marsh from the 3rd German ed., Oxford: Basil Blackwell, and New York: Harper and Row, 1963.

— *Theology of the New Testament,* trans. Kendrick Grobel, Vol. I, New York: Charles Scribner's Sons, 1951; London: SCM Press, 1952.

Burkill, T. Alec, *Mysterious Revelation: An Examination of the Philosophy of St Mark's Gospel,* Ithaca, N.Y.: Cornell University Press, 1963.

Butler, Basil C., *The Originality of St Matthew,* Cambridge: Cambridge University Press, 1951.

Coleman, N. D., 'Some Noteworthy Uses of εἰ or εἶ in Hellenistic Greek, with a Note on St Mark 8.12', *JTS* XXVIII (1927), 159–67.

Conzelmann, Hans, *An* **Outline** *of the Theology of the New Testament,* trans. John Bowden from the 2nd German ed., London: SCM Press, and New York: Harper and Row, 1969.

— *The Theology of St Luke,* trans. Geoffrey Buswell from the 2nd German ed. of *Die Mitte der Zeit,* London: Faber and Faber, 1960; New York: Harper and Row, 1961.

Cullmann, Oscar, **Salvation** *in History,* trans. S. G. Sowers, London: SCM Press, and New York: Harper and Row, 1967.

Delling, Gerhard, 'τρεῖς, τρίς, τρίτος', *TWNT* VIII, 1969, 215–25.

Dibelius, Martin, *From* **Tradition** *to Gospel,* trans. in collaboration with the author by Bertram Lee Woolf from the revised 2nd German ed., London: Nicholson and Watson, 1934; New York: Charles Scribner's Sons, 1935.

— *Gospel Criticism and Christology,* London: Nicholson and Watson, 1935.

Dobschütz, Ernst von, *Vom Auslegung des Neuen Testaments,* Göttingen: Vandenhoeck und Ruprecht, 1927.

Downing, F. G., 'Toward the Rehabilitation of Q', *NTS* XI (1964–65), 169–81.

Farmer, William, *The Synoptic Problem,* New York: Macmillan, 1964.

Feine, Paul, Behm, Johannes, and **Kümmel,** Werner Georg, **Introduction** *to the New Testament,* trans. A. J. Mattill, from the 14th revised German ed., Nashville, Tenn.: Abingdon Press, and London: SCM Press, 1966.

Filson, Floyd V., *A Commentary on the Gospel According to St Matthew,* London: Adam and Charles Black, and New York: Harper and Row, 1960.

Fitzmyer, Joseph A., S. J., 'The Priority of Mark and the "Q" Source in Luke', *Jesus and Man's Hope,* Vol. I, Pittsburgh: Pittsburgh Theological Seminary, 1970.

Fuller, Reginald H., *The Foundations of New Testament Christology,* New York: Charles Scribner's Sons, and London: Lutterworth, 1965.

Gaechter, Paul, *Das Matthäus Evangelium,* Innsbruck: Tyrolia-Verlag, 1963.

Gerhardsson, B., *Memory and Manuscript: Oral Tradition and Written Transmission in Rabbinic Judaism and Early Christianity,* trans. Eric Sharpe (ASNU 22), 1961.

Ginsberg, Louis, *Legends of the Jews,* 6 vols., Philadelphia: Jewish Publication Society of America, 1938.

Glombitza, Otto, 'Das Zeichen des Jona (Zum Verständnis von Matthäus 12.38–42)', *NTS* VIII (1962), 359–66.

Lagrange, M.-J., *Evangile selon Saint Matthieu,* Paris: Lecoffre, 1923.

Haenchen, Ernst, *Die Apostelgeschichte,* 5th ed., Göttingen: Vandenhoeck und Ruprecht, 1965.

— *Der Weg Jesu: Eine Erklärung des Markus-Evangeliums und der kanonischen Parallelen,* Berlin: Alfred Töpelmann, 1966.

Hahn, Ferdinand, *Christologische Hoheitstitel: Ihre Geschichte in Frühen Christentum* (FRLANT 83), 3rd ed., 1966.

Harnack, Adolf, *The* **Sayings** *of Jesus,* trans. J. R. Wilkenson, London: Williams and Norgate, 1908.

Holtzmann, Heinrich J., *Die Synoptiker* (Hand-Commentar zum Neuen Testament, Vol. I), Freiburg I. B.: J. C. B. Mohr, 1892.

— *Die synoptischen Evangelien: Ihr Ursprung und geschichtlicher Charakter,* Leipzig: W. Engelmann, 1863.

Hooker, Morna D., *The Son of Man in Mark,* London: SPCK, and Montreal: McGill University Press, 1967.

Howton, Dom John, 'The Sign of Jonah', *SJT* XV (1962), 288–304.

Hunt, B. P. W. Stather, *Primitive Gospel Sources,* London: James Clarke, and New York: Philosophical Library, 1951.

Jeremias, Joachim, 'Μωυσῆς', *TWNT*, IV, 1943, 852–78; *TDNT* IV, 1967, 848–73.

—'Ἰωνᾶς', *TWNT* III, 1938, 410–13; *TDNT* III, 1965, 406–10.

Joüon, Paul, *Grammaire de l'Hébreu biblique,* Rome: Institute Biblique Pontificale, 1923.

Käsemann, Ernst, 'The Beginnings of Christian Theology', *New Testament Questions of Today,* trans. W. J. Montague, London: SCM Press, and Philadelphia: Fortress Press, 1969, 82–107.

— 'Sentences of Holy Law in the New Testament', *ibid.,* 66–81.

— 'On the Subject of Primitive Christian Apocalyptic', *ibid.,* 108–38.

Kautzsch, Emil (ed.), *Gesenius' Hebrew Grammar,* translated by A. E. Cowley, Oxford: Clarendon Press, 1910.

Keck, Leander, and Martyn, J. Louis (eds.), *Studies in Luke-Acts: Essays presented in honor of Paul Schubert,* Nashville, Tenn.: Abingdon Press, 1966.

Kilpatrick, George Dunbar, *The Origins of the Gospel according to St Matthew,* Oxford: Clarendon Press, 1946.

Klostermann, Erich, *Matthäus* (Handbuch zum Neuen Testament II), Tübingen: J. C. B. Mohr, 1909.

Knigge, Heinz-Dieter, 'The Meaning of **Mark**: the Exegesis of the Second Gospel', *Interpretation* XXII (1968), 53–70.

Kramer, Werner, *Christ, Lord, Son of God,* trans. Brian Hardy, (SBT 50), 1966.

Lindars, Barnabas, *New Testament Apologetic: the Doctrinal Significance of the Old Testament Quotations,* London: SCM Press, and Philadelphia: Westminster Press, 1961.

Linton, Olaf, 'The Demand for a Sign from Heaven (Mark 8.11–12 and par.)', *Studia Theologica* XIX (1965), 112–29.

Lohmeyer, Ernst, and Schmauch, Werner, *Das Evangelium des Matthäus*, Göttingen: Vandenhoeck und Ruprecht, 1956.

McKnight, Edgar V., *What is Form Criticism?* (Guides to Biblical Scholarship), Philadelphia: Fortress Press, 1969.

McNeile, Alan Hugh, *The Gospel According to St Matthew*, London: Macmillan, 1915.

Manson, T. W., *The Sayings of Jesus*, London: SCM Press, and Toronto: Ryerson Press, 1949 (Part Two of H. D. A. Major, T. W. Manson and C. J. Wright, *The Mission and Message of Jesus*, London: Nicholson and Watson, 1937).

Marxsen, Willi, *Der Evangelist Markus: Studien zur Redaktionsgeschichte des Evangeliums* (FRLANT 67), 2nd ed., 1959.

*Mekilta de-Rabbi Ishmael*, ed. J. Z. Lauterbach, 3 vols., Philadelphia: Jewish Publication Society of America, 1949.

Meyer, Paul D., *The Community of Q*, Unpublished Ph.D. dissertation, University of Iowa, 1967.

Michael, J. H., 'The Sign of John', *JTS* XXI (1920), 146–59.

*Midrash Rabbah,* ed. H. Freedman and M. Simon, 10 vols., London: Soncino Press, 1939.

*Mishnah,* ed. Philip Blackman, 7 vols., London: Macmillan, 1951–56.

Montefiore, C. G., *The Synoptic Gospels,* Vol. II, London: Macmillan, 1927.

Moulton, W. F., and Geden, A. S., *A Concordance to the Greek New Testament,* Edinburgh: T. & T. Clark, and New York: Charles Scribner's Sons, 1897.

Moulton, James Hope, *A Grammar of New Testament Greek,* Vol. III: *Syntax,* by Nigel Turner, Edinburgh: T. and T. Clark, 1963.

Moxon, C. 'τὸ σημεῖον Ἰωνᾶ'. *ExpT* XXII (1911), 566f.

Nepper-Christensen, Poul, *Das Matthäusevangelium. Ein judenchristliches Evangelium?*, Aarhus: Universitetsforlaget, 1958.

Perrin, Norman, **Rediscovering** *the Teaching of Jesus* (NTL), 1967.
— 'The **Son of Man** in the Synoptic Tradition', Paper presented at the annual meeting of the Society of Biblical Literature in New York on 27 December 1967. (Mimeographed.)
—*What is* **Redaction Criticism?** (Guides to Biblical Scholarship), Philadelphia: Fortress Press, 1969.

Petrie, Stewart, '"Q" is only what you make it', *Novum Testamentum* III (1959), 28–33.

Plummer, Alfred, *An Exegetical Commentary on the Gospel According to St Matthew,* London: Eliot Stock, and New York: Charles Scribner's Sons, 1909.

Rengstorf, Karl, 'σημεῖον', *TWNT* VII, 1964, pp. 199–261.

Robinson, James M., 'ΛΟΓΟΙ ΣΟΦΩΝ: Zur Gattung der Spruchquelle Q', *Zeit und Geschichte: Dankesgabe an R. Bultmann zum 80. Geburtstag,* ed. E. Dinkler, Tübingen: J. C. B. Mohr, 1964.

— *The Problem of History in Mark* (SBT 21), 1957.

Rohde, Joachim, **Rediscovering** *the Teaching of the Evangelists,* trans. Dorothea M. Barton (NTL), 1968.

Rosché, Theodore R., 'The Words of Jesus and the Future of the Q Hypothesis', *JBL* LXXIX (1960), 210–20.

Schlatter, Adolf, *Der Evangelist Matthäus,* Stuttgart: Calwer Verlag, 1948.

Schmid, Josef, *Das Evangelium Matthäus* (Regensberger Neues Testament, Vol. I), Regensberg: Pustet, 1959.

Schmidt, Karl Ludwig, *Der Rahmen der Geschichte Jesu,* Berlin: Trowitzsch und Sohn, 1919.

Seidelin, Paul, 'Das Jonaszeichen', *Studia Theologica* V (1952), 119–31.

Steffen, Uwe, *Das Mysterium von Tod und Auferstehung: Formen und Wandlungen des Jona-Motivs,* Göttingen: Vandenhoeck und Ruprecht, 1963.

Stendahl, Krister, *The School of St* **Matthew** – *and its Use of the Old Testament* (ASNU 20), 1954.

Strecker, Georg, 'The Concept of History in Matthew,' *JAAR* XXXV (1967), 219–30.

— *Der Weg der Gerechtigkeit. Untersuchungen zur Theologie des Matthäus* (FRLANT 82), 1962.

Streeter, B. H., *The Four Gospels: A Study of Origins,* London: Macmillan, 1926.

*Le Talmud de Jerusalem,* 11 vols., trans. Moïse Schwab, Paris: J. Maisonneuve, 1890.

Taylor, Vincent, *The Gospel According to St Mark,* 2nd ed., London: Macmillan, 1966.

— 'The Original Order of Q', *New Testament Essays: Studies in Memory of T. W. Manson,* ed. A. J. Higgins, Manchester: University of Manchester Press, 1959.

Throckmorton, Burton H., 'Did Mark know Q?', *JBL* LXVII (1948), 319–29.

Tödt, Heinz Eduard, *The Son of Man in the Synoptic Tradition,* trans. Dorothea M. Barton, London: SCM Press, 1965.

Trilling, Wolfgang, *Das Wahre Israel,* 3rd ed., München: Kösel-Verlag, 1964.

Vielhauer, Philipp, 'Gottesreich und Menschensohn in der Verkündigung Jesu', *Festschrift für Günther Dehn,* ed. W. Schneemelcher, Neukirchen: Verlag der Buchhandlung des Erziehungsvereins Neukirchen, 1957.

— 'Jesus und der Menschensohn: Zur Diskussion mit Heinz Eduard Tödt und Eduard Schweizer', *ZThK* LX (1963), 133–77.

Vögtle, Anton, 'Der Spruch vom **Jonaszeichen**', *Synoptische Studien: Alfred Wikenhauser zum siebzigsten Geburtstag am 22. Februar 1953 dargebracht von Freunden, Kollegen und Schülern,* München: Karl Zink Verlag, 1953.

Weeden, T. J., *The Heresy that Necessitated Mark's Gospel,* Unpublished dissertation at Claremont Graduate School, Claremont, California, 1967.

Wellhausen, Julius, *Einleitung in die drei ersten Evangelien,* Berlin: G. Reimer, 1905.

— *Das Evangelium Matthae,* Berlin: G. Reimer, 1904.

Westcott, Brooke Foss, and Hort, Fenton John, *The New Testament in the Original Greek.* Vol. II: *Introduction and Appendix,* Cambridge and London: Macmillan, and New York: Harper and Bros., 1882.

Wilson, R. McL., *Studies in the Gospel of Thomas,* London: Mowbray, 1960.

Wrede, William, *Das Messiasgeheimnis in der Evangelien. Zugleich ein Beitrag zum Verständnis des Markus-evangeliums,* Göttingen: Vandenhoeck und Ruprecht, 1901.

# INDEX OF NAMES

# INDEX OF BIBLICAL REFERENCES